Blockchain with Elixir

I0477611

A Developer's Guide for Building High-Performance Blockchain Network

Frank Nowlin

Table of Contents

Preface

Hey there, Are you intrigued by the potential of blockchain technology? Do you want to be part of the next wave of innovation, building secure and powerful applications that change the way we interact and transact? If you're nodding your head (or tapping your foot impatiently!), then this book is for you!

Background and Motivation

The world is buzzing with excitement about blockchain. This revolutionary technology is shaking things up in finance, supply chain management, even voting systems. But here's the thing: building secure and scalable blockchain applications requires the right tools.

That's where Elixir comes in. This fantastic functional programming language shines with features like concurrency, fault tolerance, and a clean, concise syntax. In short, it's perfect for building high-performance, reliable blockchain applications.

Now, I know what you're thinking: "Great, but where do I start?"

This book is your roadmap. It's designed to be clear, engaging, and informative, whether you're a seasoned developer or just starting your blockchain adventure.

Purpose and Scope

This book aims to equip you with the knowledge and skills to build your own blockchain applications using Elixir. We'll break things down step-by-step, starting with the core concepts of blockchain technology. You'll learn how transactions are recorded securely, how consensus mechanisms work, and how smart contracts enable trustless interactions.

But this book isn't just about theory. We'll dive right into the practical side of things. You'll build your own blockchain node, implement consensus algorithms, and learn best practices for securing your applications. Along the way, we'll explore the benefits of using Elixir for blockchain development, taking advantage of its strengths to build robust and scalable systems.

Target Audience

This book is for anyone who wants to learn how to build blockchain applications with Elixir. Whether you're a beginner programmer eager to explore this exciting new technology, or an experienced developer looking to add blockchain to your skillset, you'll find valuable information here.

We'll assume you have some basic programming experience, but no prior knowledge of blockchain is required. We'll break down complex concepts into clear, easy-to-understand explanations.

Organization and Structure

This book is structured to take you on a smooth learning curve. We've divided it into three parts:

- Part 1: Foundations (Chapters 1-3) - We'll get you acquainted with Elixir programming and provide a solid understanding of blockchain fundamentals.
- Part 2: Building Blocks (Chapters 4-8) - Here's where things get hands-on! We'll equip you with the practical skills to build your own blockchain node, implement consensus mechanisms, and ensure the security of your applications.
- Part 3: Advanced Topics (Chapters 9-10) - Ready to see blockchain in action? We'll build a real-world application – a cryptocurrency! We'll also explore decentralized applications (dApps) to solidify your understanding.

Invitation to Read

So, are you ready to unlock the power of blockchain development with Elixir? Let's roll up our sleeves and start building! This book is packed with clear explanations, practical examples, and a dash of enthusiasm to keep you motivated. By the end, you'll be well on your way to becoming a confident blockchain developer, ready to contribute to the future of technology. Let's dive in!

Introduction

This book, "Blockchain with Elixir: A Developer's Guide for Building High-Performance Blockchain Networks," is designed to equip you with the knowledge and skills to build secure and scalable blockchain applications using the Elixir programming language. Whether you're a seasoned developer or just starting your exploration of blockchain technology, this guide will provide a clear and comprehensive roadmap.

What is Blockchain?

A blockchain is a distributed ledger technology that securely records transactions across a network of computers. Imagine a shared spreadsheet, but instead of being stored on a single server controlled by one entity, a blockchain is replicated and maintained by all participants in the network. This distributed nature offers several key advantages:

- Immutability: Once a transaction is added to a blockchain, it cannot be altered or deleted. This creates a permanent and tamper-proof record of all activity on the network.
- Transparency: All participants in the network have access to the complete transaction history, fostering trust and accountability.
- Decentralization: There is no central authority controlling the network. This eliminates the need for a trusted third party and reduces the risk of single points of failure.

These characteristics make blockchain a powerful technology for a wide range of applications, including:

- Cryptocurrencies: Digital currencies like Bitcoin and Ethereum are built on blockchain technology.
- Supply Chain Management: Blockchain can be used to track the movement of goods and materials throughout a supply chain, ensuring transparency and efficiency.
- Voting Systems: Blockchain-based voting systems can improve security and reduce the risk of fraud.
- Identity Management: Blockchain can provide a secure and tamper-proof way to store and manage personal identity information.

Why Elixir for Blockchain?

Elixir is a functional programming language known for its concurrency, scalability, and fault tolerance. These features make it a strong contender for developing high-performance blockchain applications. Here's how Elixir benefits blockchain development:

- Concurrency: Blockchain networks involve a high volume of transactions. Elixir's concurrency capabilities allow developers to efficiently handle multiple tasks simultaneously, leading to faster and more responsive applications.
- Scalability: As the number of users on a blockchain network grows, the system needs to be able to handle the increased load. Elixir's design promotes

scalability, ensuring your applications can adapt to future demands.

- Fault Tolerance: Blockchain networks should be resilient to failures. Elixir's built-in fault tolerance mechanisms help ensure that your applications can continue to operate even if individual nodes experience problems.

Beyond these technical advantages, Elixir offers a clean and concise syntax, making it easier to write maintainable and bug-free code. Additionally, the Elixir community is actively developing libraries and tools specifically for blockchain development.

Chapter 1: Introduction to Elixir

Alright, In this chapter, we'll be setting the stage for your journey into building blockchain applications with Elixir. Think of it as grabbing your toolbox and making sure all the cool gadgets are there before we start building something awesome.

1.1 History and Background

Elixir is a relatively young programming language compared to some established giants. However, it boasts a strong lineage, inheriting core functionalities from its predecessor, Erlang. Developed by Ericsson in the 1980s, Erlang was specifically designed for building robust and fault-tolerant systems – ideal for critical tasks like managing telecommunication networks.

Here's a key point: while Erlang excelled in reliability, its syntax – the way instructions are written – could be challenging to learn and read. This is where Elixir comes in. Created in 2012, Elixir took the powerful core of Erlang and wrapped it in a cleaner, more readable syntax. Imagine Erlang receiving a significant upgrade in terms of user-friendliness for developers.

But why is Elixir particularly well-suited for blockchain development? The answer lies in the features it inherited from Erlang:

- Concurrency: Blockchain networks involve a high volume of transactions happening simultaneously. Concurrency refers to a program's ability to handle multiple tasks at once. Elixir excels in this area, allowing developers to efficiently manage the constant flow of transactions within a blockchain application.
- Scalability: As your blockchain application gains traction and attracts more users, it needs to handle the increased demand. Scalability refers to a system's ability to adapt and grow efficiently. Elixir's design promotes scalability, ensuring your applications can handle future growth without compromising performance.
- Fault Tolerance: Unexpected issues can arise in any system. Fault tolerance refers to a system's ability to remain operational even if individual components experience problems. Elixir's built-in fault tolerance mechanisms help guarantee that your applications can continue to function smoothly even if certain parts encounter hiccups.

In essence, Elixir combines a clear and concise syntax with the power to handle the complexities inherent in blockchain development. This makes it a compelling choice for building secure and scalable blockchain applications.

1.2 Setting Up the Elixir Development Environment

Now that you're excited about using Elixir for blockchain development, let's set up your development environment. Think of it as building your personalized coding workspace for creating awesome blockchain applications. Here's what you'll need:

1. Download Elixir and Erlang: Head over to the official Elixir website (https://elixir-lang.org/install.html) and grab the latest installer for your operating system. Don't worry, Erlang typically comes bundled with Elixir, so you're getting both tools in one download!

2. Open Your Terminal: This is your command center where you'll communicate with Elixir directly. On Windows, it's likely called Command Prompt, while macOS and Linux users can use the Terminal application.

3. Test It Out: Open your terminal and type iex. If you see "Interactive Elixir (iex) 1.x.x" pop up, congratulations! That means Elixir is installed correctly and ready to take your commands.

4. Bonus Tip: While you can code directly in iex, most developers prefer using a code editor or IDE (Integrated Development Environment). These tools offer features like syntax highlighting, code completion, and debugging, making your development process much smoother. Popular options for Elixir development include Visual Studio Code with the ElixirLS plugin or Emacs with the Alchemist mode.

Awesome! You've successfully set up your Elixir development environment. Now you have the tools you need to start building your blockchain dreams.

Here are some additional details that might be helpful:

- Understanding Installers: Installers are programs that guide you through the installation process of software. They typically handle downloading the necessary files, configuring settings, and integrating the software with your system.
- Interactive Elixir (iex): This is a built-in tool in Elixir that allows you to interact with the language directly in your terminal. It's a great way to test code snippets or experiment with basic functionalities.

By following these steps, you'll have your development environment ready to start writing Elixir code and exploring the exciting world of blockchain development.

1.3 Basic Syntax and Features of Elixir

Elixir might seem like a foreign language at first, but don't worry! We'll break down its core concepts into manageable pieces. Here are some fundamental elements you'll encounter as you build your blockchain applications with Elixir:

1. Functions:

Imagine functions as mini-programs within your code. They take inputs (arguments) and produce outputs (results). These functions are the building blocks you'll use to construct all the various parts of your blockchain applications.

Here's a simple example of a function that adds two numbers:

```elixir
Elixir
def add(x, y) do
  x + y
end
result = add(5, 3)
IO.puts result  # This will print "8" to the console
```

In this example:
- def defines a function named add.
- x and y are the arguments (inputs) the function takes.
- x + y is the expression that calculates the sum.
- end marks the end of the function definition.
- result = add(5, 3) calls the add function with arguments 5 and 3, storing the result in the variable result.
- IO.puts result prints the value of result (which is 8) to the console.

2. Pattern Matching

Pattern matching is a unique way Elixir checks if data matches a specific format. Think of it like a puzzle – you need to fit the pieces together just right. It allows for more concise and readable code compared to traditional conditional statements found in other languages.

Here's an example of pattern matching to check if a number is even or odd:

```elixir
Elixir
def even_or_odd(number) do
 cond do
  number rem 2 == 0 -> IO.puts "Even"
  true -> IO.puts "Odd"
 end
end
even_or_odd(10)  # This will print "Even"
even_or_odd(7)   # This will print "Odd"
```

In this example:
- cond is a construct for pattern matching.
- number rem 2 == 0 checks if the remainder of dividing number by 2 is 0 (indicating an even number).
- true acts as a catch-all for any number that doesn't match the first pattern (meaning it's odd).
- IO.puts prints the corresponding message based on the matched pattern.

3. Processes and OTP: Handling Concurrent Tasks Efficiently

Elixir excels at managing concurrent tasks – meaning it can handle multiple things happening at once. This is crucial for blockchain applications that constantly process transactions. Processes are like individual actors in your application, each running independently.

OTP (Open Telecom Platform) is a set of tools included with Elixir that helps you manage and coordinate these processes. It provides features for starting, stopping, and monitoring processes, ensuring your application runs smoothly even with multiple tasks happening concurrently.

These are just a stepping stone! As we delve deeper into the book, you'll explore more advanced concepts of Elixir and how they empower you to build robust and scalable blockchain applications.

Chapter 2: Blockchain Fundamentals

In this chapter, we'll crack open the mysterious world of blockchain technology. We'll break down how it works, explore different types of blockchains, and unveil the key components that make it all tick.

2.1 How Blockchain Works

Blockchain technology has taken the world by storm, but its inner workings might seem a bit mysterious. This section will shed light on how blockchain operates, breaking down the core concepts into clear and understandable terms.

Imagine a secure and transparent ledger, not unlike a giant spreadsheet, but with a crucial twist: it's not stored on a single server controlled by one entity. Instead, this ledger is replicated and maintained by a network of computers distributed across the globe. This distributed nature is the essence of blockchain technology.

Here's a step-by-step breakdown of how transactions are recorded securely and transparently on a blockchain:

1. Transactions Occur: Let's say Sarah wants to send 10 digital coins to David on the blockchain network. This transaction is broadcast to all participants in the

network, ensuring everyone is aware of the intended transfer.

2. Blocks Take Shape: These broadcasted transactions are bundled together into a digital container called a "block." Think of it as a page in the shared ledger, holding a collection of verified transactions.

3. Miners Secure the Network: Special computers on the network, called "miners," compete to solve a complex mathematical puzzle. The first miner to solve the puzzle gets to add their block, containing the bundled transactions, to the ever-growing chain. This process is called "mining" and serves as a security measure.

4. The Chain Grows Stronger: Each newly added block includes a unique cryptographic reference (a hash) to the block before it. This creates a chronological chain – tampering with any block would require altering all subsequent blocks, making it nearly impossible to manipulate the record.

5. Transparency for All: Since every participant on the network has a copy of the entire blockchain, complete transparency is achieved. All transactions are visible to everyone, fostering trust and accountability.

Key Advantages of Blockchain Technology:

- Enhanced Security: The distributed nature of the ledger and the use of cryptography make it extremely difficult to tamper with data on a blockchain.
- Unmatched Transparency: Everyone on the network can see all transactions, promoting trust and reducing the risk of fraud.

- Immutable Record-Keeping: Once a transaction is added to a blockchain, it cannot be altered or deleted, guaranteeing a permanent and verifiable record.

This simplified explanation provides a foundational understanding of how blockchain technology operates. As we delve deeper in this book, we'll explore the technical details behind mining, cryptography, and various consensus mechanisms that further solidify the security and integrity of blockchain networks.

2.2 Types of Blockchains

The exciting world of blockchain offers a variety of options to suit different needs. Just like clothes come in various styles, blockchains have different structures depending on their intended use. Here's a breakdown of the three main types of blockchains:

Public Blockchains: Open and Permissionless

Imagine a vibrant public park — anyone can enter, participate in activities, and witness everything that happens. Public blockchains operate in a similar fashion. They are open and permissionless, meaning:

- Open Participation: There are no barriers to entry. Anyone with an internet connection and the necessary software can join the network, participate in transactions, and even become a miner.

- Transparency Reigns Supreme: The entire blockchain ledger, including all transactions, is publicly accessible for everyone to view. This fosters trust and accountability within the network.
- Security Through Decentralization: The distributed nature of public blockchains, with multiple copies of the ledger held by participants, makes them highly resistant to attacks or manipulation.

Popular examples of public blockchains include Bitcoin and Ethereum. These networks are often used for:

- Decentralized Finance (DeFi): Enabling peer-to-peer financial transactions without the need for intermediaries.
- Cryptocurrencies: Facilitating the secure transfer and ownership of digital currencies.
- Non-Fungible Tokens (NFTs): Providing a secure and transparent way to represent unique digital assets.

Private Blockchains: Permissioned and Controlled

Think of a private club with exclusive access. Private blockchains are permissioned networks, meaning:

- Controlled Access: A single organization or group controls who can join and participate in the network. This allows them to determine who can add transactions and validate them.
- Enhanced Scalability: Since the number of participants is limited, private blockchains can

potentially process transactions faster and more efficiently compared to public blockchains.

- Focus on Control: Organizations can tailor the rules and functionalities of the private blockchain to meet their specific needs.

Private blockchains are often used for:

- Supply Chain Management: Tracking the movement of goods and materials throughout a supply chain with greater transparency and security.
- Healthcare Data Management: Sharing sensitive patient data securely among authorized healthcare providers.
- Voting Systems: Enhancing the security and integrity of voting processes.

Consortium Blockchains

Imagine a group project where several trusted entities work together. Consortium blockchains operate on a similar principle:

- Multiple Organizations Participate: A consortium blockchain is shared by a pre-selected group of trusted entities, offering a balance between the openness of public blockchains and the control of private ones.
- Focus on Shared Goals: The participating organizations typically have a common interest or business goal that the blockchain helps to facilitate.

- Enhanced Efficiency: By limiting access to trusted participants, consortium blockchains can achieve faster transaction processing and improved scalability compared to public blockchains.

Consortium blockchains are often used for:
- Trade Finance: Streamlining trade finance processes between banks and other financial institutions.
- Identity Management: Creating a secure and collaborative system for managing user identities across different organizations.

The choice of blockchain type depends on the specific needs of the application. Public blockchains excel in transparency and security for permissionless use cases, while private and consortium blockchains offer greater control and scalability for specific applications where a defined set of participants is involved.

2.3 Key Blockchain Components

Now that you understand the core concept of blockchain technology, let's zoom in on the essential ingredients that make it function:

Blocks:

Imagine a series of secure filing cabinets, each holding a collection of verified transactions. These cabinets are the blockchain's "blocks." A block typically stores the following information:

- Transaction Data: This includes details about the sender, receiver, and amount of a transaction. In some blockchains, additional data relevant to the specific application can also be included.
- Timestamp: Each block is assigned a unique timestamp, recording the exact time the block was created. This helps maintain a chronological order of transactions on the blockchain.
- Hash: Think of a hash as a unique digital fingerprint for each block. It's a complex mathematical calculation based on the block's data and the hash of the preceding block. Any alteration to the data within a block would result in a completely different hash, making it easy to detect tampering attempts.

Transactions:

Transactions are the events that keep the blockchain network humming. They represent the exchange of value between participants on the network. This value can take various forms depending on the blockchain's application:

- Digital Currency: In blockchains like Bitcoin or Ethereum, transactions represent the transfer of digital coins between users.
- Asset Ownership: Some blockchains can be used to track ownership of real-world assets, with transactions reflecting changes in ownership.
- Data Exchange: Blockchains can also be used to securely exchange data between authorized parties,

with transactions representing the data being transferred.

Consensus Mechanism

Imagine a group of people trying to reach a consensus on a decision. In a blockchain network, the consensus mechanism plays a similar role. It's the process by which all participants in the network agree on the validity of transactions and the order in which they are added to the blockchain. This is crucial for maintaining a secure and reliable shared ledger.

There are different types of consensus mechanisms, each with its own advantages and disadvantages. We'll explore some popular mechanisms like Proof of Work (PoW) and Proof of Stake (PoS) in detail later in the book.

By understanding these key components – blocks, transactions, and consensus mechanisms – you'll gain a solid foundation for building your own secure and trustworthy blockchain applications with Elixir!

Chapter 3: Setting Up Your Project

This chapter is all about getting your hands dirty and building the foundation for your awesome blockchain application! We'll be using Elixir, a powerful and readable language, to craft something truly special.

3.1 Creating a New Elixir Project with Mix

Elixir is a fantastic language for building blockchain applications, and Mix is your go-to tool for setting up and managing your project. Mix is like a Swiss Army knife for Elixir development, helping you create new projects, manage dependencies, compile code, and more. Let's get started and build the foundation for your blockchain project!

Before we dive in, make sure you have Elixir and Erlang installed on your system. Head over to the official Elixir website (https://elixir-lang.org/install.html) and grab the latest installer for your operating system. Don't worry, Erlang typically comes bundled with Elixir, so you're getting both tools in one download!

Creating a New Project:

1. Open your terminal: This is your command center for interacting with Mix. On Windows, it's likely called

Command Prompt, while macOS and Linux users can use the Terminal application.

2. Navigate to your desired project directory: Use the cd command to navigate to the location where you want to create your project. For example, if you want to create a project on your Desktop, you might type:

Bash
cd Desktop

3. Create your project: Now for the exciting part! In your terminal, type the following command, replacing "my_blockchain_app" with your desired project name:

Bash
mix new my_blockchain_app

Hit Enter, and Mix will spring into action. You'll see some output in your terminal indicating that Mix is creating the project directory structure and setting up essential files.

Project Structure:

Mix creates a new directory with a predefined structure containing all the necessary files to get you started. Here's a quick breakdown of some key folders:

- lib: This is the heart of your project, containing the Elixir code that defines how your application functions. You'll create new modules and files within this folder to build your blockchain application's logic.

- mix.exs: This file acts as the configuration center for your project. It specifies dependencies (like external libraries your project needs), defines tasks (custom actions you can run with Mix), and provides other essential settings for Mix to manage your project effectively.
- test: As the name suggests, this folder is where you'll store your test code. Writing tests is crucial for ensuring the quality and reliability of your application. We'll explore testing in more detail later.

Verifying Your Project:

Once Mix finishes creating the project, navigate into the newly created directory using the cd command:

Bash
cd my_blockchain_app

Now, try running mix in your terminal within the project directory. Mix will display a list of available tasks you can execute. This verifies that your project is set up correctly and Mix is ready to assist you in your development journey.

Compiling Your Code:

Elixir code needs to be compiled before it can be run. Mix handles this compilation process for you. To compile your project, simply run the following command in your terminal:

Bash
mix compile

This will compile all the Elixir code in your project, making it ready for execution.

Example: A Simple Hello World Application:

Let's create a basic Elixir module to get your feet wet:
1. Create a new file: Within the lib directory, create a new file named hello_blockchain.ex. This file will contain your Elixir code.
2. Define a module: Open the hello_blockchain.ex file in your favorite text editor and add the following code:

Elixir
```
defmodule HelloBlockchain do
 def greet(name) do
     IO.puts "Hello, #{name}! Welcome to the world of blockchain development!"
 end
end
```

This code defines a module named HelloBlockchain with a function called greet. The greet function takes a name as an argument and prints a friendly message to the console.

3. Run the code: Now, in your terminal within the project directory, run the following command:

Bash
iex -S mix phx.server

This command starts an interactive Elixir shell (iex) with the mix phx.server application context.

4. Interact with your code: In the interactive shell, type the following command to call the greet function from your HelloBlockchain module:

Elixir
HelloBlockchain.greet("Blockchain Enthusiast")

Hit Enter, and you should see the following output:
Hello, Blockchain Enthusiast! Welcome to the world of blockchain development! This simple example demonstrates how to create a basic Elixir module

After running HelloBlockchain.greet("Blockchain Enthusiast") in the interactive shell and seeing the output, you can experiment further with your code. Here are some ways to interact with your code:

- Try different greetings: Modify the argument passed to the greet function. For example:

Elixir
HelloBlockchain.greet("Elixir Developer")

This will print a different greeting message with the new name.

- Explore the Elixir shell: The interactive Elixir shell (iex) offers various features for exploring and experimenting with your code. Use the h or help command to get a list of available commands and functions.

- Exit the interactive shell: Once you're done experimenting, you can exit the interactive shell by typing q or quit and pressing Enter.

This was a small taste of Elixir and Mix. As you progress through this book, you'll delve deeper into building more complex blockchain applications using Elixir's powerful features and various libraries.

3.2 Essential Libraries and Dependencies

While Elixir provides a powerful core for building applications, sometimes you need additional tools for specific functionalities. This is where libraries come in – pre-written collections of code that offer reusable functionalities and extend your coding capabilities. In the context of blockchain development with Elixir, here are some essential libraries you'll likely encounter:

1. **Ecto:**

Imagine your blockchain application needs to store additional information alongside the blockchain data. This is where Ecto comes in. Ecto is a popular database library for Elixir that acts as a bridge between your application and various database systems.

Here's what Ecto offers:

- Database Interactions: Ecto provides functions and modules for interacting with databases – creating, reading, updating, and deleting data.
- Schema Definition: You can define the structure of your data using Ecto schemas. These schemas act as blueprints, specifying the types and relationships of data stored in your database.
- Database Agnosticism: While Ecto supports various database systems like PostgreSQL and MySQL, your code remains largely database-independent. This means you can switch between databases more easily if needed.

Example: Defining a Simple Ecto Schema

Let's create a basic schema to represent a user in our blockchain application:

```Elixir
defmodule MyApp.User do
  use Ecto.Schema
  schema do
    field :name, :string
    field :email, :string
  end
end
```

This code defines a schema named MyApp.User with two fields: name (a string) and email (also a string). This schema tells Ecto how to structure user data in the database.

2. BlockChain.NET

While Elixir is fantastic for building new blockchain applications, there might be situations where you want to interact with existing blockchains like Bitcoin or Ethereum. This is where BlockChain.NET comes into play.
BlockChain.NET acts as a bridge between your Elixir code and various blockchain networks. It provides functionalities for:

- Node Communication: Establish connections with blockchain network nodes to send and receive data.
- Transaction Building and Submission: Craft transactions according to the specific blockchain's format and submit them to the network for processing.
- Data Retrieval: Query the blockchain network to retrieve information about transactions, blocks, and other relevant data.

Using BlockChain.NET might require additional setup and configuration depending on the specific blockchain network you're targeting.

GenServer: Mastering Long-Running Processes and Concurrency

Blockchain involves a lot of asynchronous tasks, like processing transactions or monitoring the network. This is where GenServer shines. GenServer is a core Elixir concept that helps you manage long-running processes and concurrent tasks efficiently.

Here's how GenServer helps:

- Process Supervision: GenServer provides a framework for creating and managing processes that can run independently within your application. This allows you to handle multiple tasks simultaneously without blocking your main program.
- State Management: Processes can maintain their own internal state, allowing them to store and access data relevant to their specific tasks.
- Fault Tolerance: GenServer helps build resilient systems. If a process crashes, GenServer can restart it automatically, ensuring your application keeps running smoothly.

Example: A Simple GenServer for Processing Transactions

Here's a simplified example to illustrate the concept:

```elixir
Elixir
defmodule MyApp.TransactionProcessor do
 use GenServer
 def init(state) do
  {:ok, state}
 end
 def handle_cast({:process_transaction, data}, state) do
  # Process the transaction data here
  {:noreply, state}
 end
end
```

This code defines a GenServer named MyApp.TransactionProcessor. It can receive messages (cast in this example) containing transaction data and process them independently.

These are examples of essential libraries for building blockchain applications with Elixir. The specific libraries you'll use will depend on the functionalities of your application. As you progress through this book, you'll explore these libraries in more detail and learn how to leverage them effectively in your blockchain development journey!

3.3 Basic Project Structure and File Organization

Just like a well-organized kitchen makes cooking enjoyable, a well-structured project directory makes developing applications smoother and more efficient. In this section, we'll explore the typical file organization for Elixir projects, specifically focusing on those geared towards blockchain development.

When you create a new Elixir project using Mix (as explained in Chapter 3.1), it sets up a basic directory structure with essential folders. Here's a breakdown of the key ones:

- lib: This is the heart of your project. It holds all the core Elixir code that defines the functionalities of your application. Here's where you'll create new modules and files containing your blockchain application's logic.

- mix.exs: Think of this as the project's control center. This file acts as the configuration hub for Mix. It specifies dependencies (external libraries your project needs), defines custom tasks you can run with Mix, and provides other essential settings for Mix to manage your project effectively.
- test: As the name suggests, this folder is dedicated to your test code. Writing unit tests is crucial for ensuring the quality and reliability of your application, especially in the complex world of blockchain development. Tests help you catch bugs and ensure your code functions as expected. We'll explore testing in more detail later in the book.

Additional Folders (Optional):

Depending on the complexity of your project, you might encounter some additional folders:

- assets: This folder might store static assets used by your application, such as images or stylesheets.
- priv: This folder is intended for private data that shouldn't be included in your codebase, such as API keys or configuration files.

Example Project Structure:
Here's a breakdown of a possible project structure for a basic blockchain application:

your_project_name/
├── lib/

```
|    ├── blockchain/
|    |    ├── block.ex
|    |    ├── transaction.ex
|    |    └── blockchain_manager.ex
|    ├── application.ex
|    └── other_modules.ex
├── mix.exs
└── test/
   └── unit/
      └── blockchain_test.exs
```

- lib/blockchain: This subfolder within lib holds all the code specific to your blockchain application logic. It might contain modules for representing blocks, transactions, and a blockchain_manager module to handle managing the blockchain itself.
- lib/application.ex: This file typically defines the overall application structure and behavior. It might configure dependencies, define processes, and specify how different modules in your project interact with each other.
- test/unit/blockchain_test.exs: This file (or multiple files) would contain unit tests for your blockchain code, ensuring it functions as expected.

Benefits of Good Organization:

- Improved Maintainability: A clear and consistent structure makes it easier for you and other developers to understand and navigate the project's codebase. This is especially important as your project grows in complexity.

- Reduced Errors: By separating concerns into different modules and folders, you can reduce the chance of code conflicts and improve the overall code quality.
- Enhanced Collaboration: A well-organized project makes collaboration with other developers smoother. Everyone can easily find the relevant code sections and understand the project's overall structure.

This is a suggested structure, and you can adapt it to your specific needs and preferences. As you gain experience, you'll develop your own conventions for organizing your Elixir projects effectively.

By following these guidelines and keeping your project well-organized, you'll lay a solid foundation for building robust and maintainable blockchain applications with Elixir!

Chapter 4: Creating a Blockchain Node

In this chapter, we'll transform your basic understanding of blockchains into a real-life, code-slinging adventure. We'll be building the core component of any blockchain network – a powerful node!

Now, imagine a node as a single computer on the blockchain network. Each node plays a crucial role in maintaining the integrity and security of the entire system. But before we dive into the code, let's strategize and design our node's architecture.

4.1 Designing the Node Architecture

The foundation of any blockchain network is the individual node. Just like strong bricks are essential for a sturdy building, a well-designed node architecture is crucial for a robust and scalable blockchain. In this section, we'll explore key considerations when designing your node's architecture, keeping scalability and performance at the forefront.

Scalability:

Imagine a small-town bakery overflowing with customers. A blockchain designed for a handful of users might struggle when the user base explodes. Scalability ensures your node can handle an increasing number of users and transactions efficiently without sacrificing performance. Here are some aspects to consider for scalability:

- Data Storage: The blockchain ledger keeps track of all transactions. As the network grows, the ledger size will increase. Choosing the right data storage solution is vital. Options like databases (e.g., Ecto) can be optimized for efficient data retrieval and manipulation even with a large ledger.

Example: Leveraging Ecto for Scalable Storage (Code Snippet):

```elixir
Elixir
defmodule MyApp.Blockchain do
  use Ecto.Schema
  schema do
    field :id, :integer, primary_key: true
    field :previous_hash, :binary
    field :data, :map
    field :hash, :binary
  end
end
```

In this example, we've defined a basic Blockchain schema using Ecto. This schema represents a single block in the blockchain. The data field is a map, allowing for flexibility in storing different types of transaction data. Ecto provides functionalities for efficient querying and manipulation of these blocks, even as the blockchain grows.

- Processing Power: Validating transactions and adding new blocks require processing power. Your node's architecture should be designed to handle this workload effectively. Consider leveraging libraries or techniques for parallel processing to distribute the tasks across multiple cores or machines if needed.

Performance

In the fast-paced world of blockchain, speed matters! Here's how to optimize your node's performance:

- Efficient Data Structures: The way you structure your data can significantly impact performance. Choosing appropriate data structures for the blockchain ledger and transaction pool can lead to faster retrieval and manipulation of information.

Example: Utilizing Maps for Transaction Pool (Code Snippet):

```elixir
Elixir
defmodule MyApp.TransactionPool do
 @transactions %{}
 def add_transaction(transaction) do
  put(@transactions, transaction.id, transaction)
 end
 def get_transaction(id) do
  @transactions[id]
 end
end
```

This code snippet showcases a simple transaction pool implemented using a map (%{}). Maps offer efficient key-value lookups, allowing for quick retrieval of specific transactions based on their ID. As the number of transactions grows, maps can still provide fast access compared to iterating through a list.

- Caching Mechanisms: Imagine a restaurant keeping frequently ordered dishes pre-prepared. Caching can be used to store frequently accessed data in memory, reducing the need for constant database queries and improving response times.
- Asynchronous Processing: Not all tasks need to be done sequentially. By implementing asynchronous processing, your node can handle multiple tasks concurrently, improving overall responsiveness.

Balancing Act: Scalability vs. Decentralization

There's a trade-off to consider. Highly centralized systems can be very scalable, but they sacrifice the core principle of decentralization that makes blockchains so powerful. Our goal is to achieve a balance – a scalable architecture that maintains the decentralized nature of the blockchain.

Core Components of a Blockchain Node:

Now that we understand the key considerations, let's delve into the core components that make up a typical blockchain node:

- Blockchain Ledger: This is the heart of the blockchain, holding a permanent and tamper-proof record of all transactions that have ever occurred on the network. Your node will need a mechanism to store and manage the ledger efficiently.

- Transaction Pool: Think of this as a waiting area for transactions. New transactions are added to the pool and wait for validation before being included in a block. The design of your transaction pool should allow for efficient addition, removal, and retrieval of transactions.
- Validation Engine: Not just any transaction can join the party! The validation engine acts as a gatekeeper, ensuring each transaction adheres to the blockchain's rules and is legitimate before adding it to a block.
- Networking Components: A lone wolf doesn't make a pack. Nodes need to communicate with each other to exchange information, synchronize data, and collaborate on maintaining the network. Your node's architecture should include functionalities for sending and receiving data to other nodes on the network.

Example: Sending and Receiving Messages with GenServer (Code Snippet):

```
Elixir
defmodule MyApp.PeerNode do
 use GenServer
 def init(state) do
  {:ok, state}
 end
 def handle_cast({:broadcast_block, block}, state) do
  # Send the block to other connected nodes
```

```
   send_message(other_nodes, {:new_block, block})
  {:noreply, state}
 end
 defp send_message(nodes, message) do
  Enum.each(nodes, fn node ->
   GenServer.cast(node, message)
  end)
 end
end
```

This example showcases a simplified GenServer process (MyApp.PeerNode) that can be used for communication between nodes. The handle_cast function demonstrates how a message to broadcast a new block ({:broadcast_block, block}) can be received. The send_message function sends the message containing the new block ({:new_block, block}) to other connected nodes using GenServer.cast.

The specific design choices for your node's architecture will depend on the type of blockchain you're building and the desired functionalities. However, by keeping scalability and performance in mind, you'll lay a solid foundation for a robust and efficient blockchain node.

Additional Considerations:

- Security: Security is paramount in any blockchain system. Your node's architecture should incorporate security measures to protect against malicious attacks and ensure the integrity of the blockchain data.

- Maintainability: As your blockchain project grows, it's crucial to consider maintainability. A well-designed and documented architecture will be easier to understand, modify, and troubleshoot in the future.

By carefully considering these factors, you will design a node architecture that is not only scalable and performant but also secure and maintainable, laying the groundwork for a powerful and robust blockchain application.

4.2 Implementing Node Functionalities

We've designed the architecture for our blockchain node, focusing on scalability and performance. Now, it's time to bring this blueprint to life by implementing the core functionalities that make it tick. Here, we'll delve into the essential functions a robust blockchain node should possess.

1. Block Validation:

Imagine a bouncer at a club, meticulously checking IDs and ensuring only eligible patrons enter. Similarly, a node's validation engine acts as a vigilant gatekeeper for the blockchain. Its role is to scrutinize each block before it gets added to the ever-growing chain. Here's what the validation engine might check:

- Cryptographic Hashes: Blockchains rely heavily on cryptography for security. Each block contains a cryptographic hash, a unique fingerprint of the block's data. The validation engine ensures the hash is calculated correctly and reflects the block's contents accurately.
- Transaction Validity: Not just any transaction can waltz in. The validation engine verifies each transaction within a block, ensuring it adheres to the blockchain's specific rules. This might involve checking digital signatures, verifying balances, and ensuring the transaction format is valid.
- Chain Consistency: A healthy blockchain is a consistent one. The validation engine ensures the new block's hash references the hash of the previous block, maintaining the chain's integrity.

Example: Simplified Block Validation (Code Snippet):

```elixir
Elixir
defmodule MyApp.BlockValidator do
  def validate_block(block) do
    # Check if the block hash is valid based on its content
    is_valid_hash?(block.hash, block.data) &&
    # Check if all transactions in the block are valid
    Enum.all?(block.transactions, &validate_transaction/1) &&
    # Check if the block references the correct previous block hash
    block.previous_hash == get_previous_block_hash()
  end
```

```
  # Implementations for is_valid_hash?,
validate_transaction, and get_previous_block_hash
omitted for brevity
end
```

This snippet showcases a simplified BlockValidator module. The validate_block function outlines the core checks – verifying the block hash, validating transactions within the block, and ensuring the chain's consistency by checking the previous block hash.

2. Transaction Processing:

Transactions are the lifeblood of any blockchain. Our node needs a system to handle incoming transactions efficiently. Here's the transaction processing workflow:

- Receiving Transactions: The node listens for incoming transactions broadcast by other nodes on the network. These transactions might be sent by users or other applications interacting with the blockchain.

Example: Using GenServer for Receiving Transactions (Code Snippet):

```
Elixir
defmodule MyApp.PeerNode do
 use GenServer
 def init(state) do
  {:ok, state, subscribe_to_transaction_topic()}
 end
```

```elixir
  def handle_info({:transaction_received, transaction},
state) do
    # Add the transaction to the pool (already implemented
in previous example)
    add_transaction_to_pool(transaction)
    {:noreply, state}
  end
  defp subscribe_to_transaction_topic() do
    # Subscribe to a topic (or mechanism) for receiving
transactions on the network
    # Specific implementation depends on the chosen
blockchain platform
  end
end
```

This code snippet expands on the PeerNode GenServer, showcasing how it can be used for receiving transactions. The init function now includes subscribing to a topic (or mechanism) for receiving transactions on the network (specific implementation details will vary depending on the chosen platform). The handle_info function demonstrates how a received transaction ({:transaction_received, transaction}) can be processed, potentially adding it to the pool using the previously implemented add_transaction_to_pool function.

- Validation: Once received, the transaction enters the waiting room – the transaction pool. The validation engine, as discussed earlier, meticulously examines the transaction to ensure its legitimacy.

Example: Utilizing Cryptographic Libraries for Transaction Validation (Code Snippet):

```elixir
Elixir
defmodule MyApp.TransactionValidator do
  def validate_transaction(transaction) do
    # Check digital signatures using a cryptographic library
(e.g., :cryptoex)
    is_valid_signature?(transaction.sender,
transaction.signature, transaction.data) &&
    # Additional validation checks specific to the blockchain
platform (e.g., sufficient funds)
    # ...
  end
  defp is_valid_signature?(public_key, signature, data) do
    # Use :cryptoex library function to verify the signature
    CryptoEx.verify(:ed25519, signature, data, public_key)
  end
end
```

This snippet showcases a TransactionValidator module. The validate_transaction function demonstrates using a cryptographic library (e.g., :cryptoex in Elixir) to verify the digital signature of a transaction. This ensures the transaction originated from the claimed sender and the data hasn't been tampered with.

- Selection for Block Inclusion: When it's time to create a new block, the node selects a set of valid transactions from the pool to include. This selection process might involve different strategies depending on the chosen blockchain platform.

Example: Simple Transaction Selection Strategy (Code Snippet):

```elixir
Elixir
defmodule MyApp.BlockBuilder do
  def select_transactions(pool) do
    # Simple strategy: select a limited number of highest-fee transactions
    Enum.take_while(pool |> Enum.sort_by(& &1.fee), fn _ -> true end, max_transactions)
  end
end
```

This example showcases a basic BlockBuilder module. The select_transactions function demonstrates a simple strategy for selecting transactions for a new block. It sorts the transactions in the pool by their fee (assuming the blockchain uses fees) and selects a limited number of the highest-fee transactions. This is a simplified approach, and more sophisticated strategies might be employed in real-world blockchain implementations.

3. Communication:

Our nodes can't operate in isolation! It needs to communicate with other nodes to exchange information, synchronize data, and collaborate on maintaining the network. Here are some crucial communication aspects for a node:

- Broadcasting Blocks: Once a node creates a new block, it broadcasts it to other nodes on the network.

This ensures everyone has the same copy of the blockchain ledger and maintains a consistent state.

- Receiving Blocks: Our node needs to listen for and receive new blocks broadcast by other nodes. This allows it to continuously update its local copy of the blockchain and stay synchronized with the network.
- Transaction Gossiping: Imagine juicy gossip spreading through a town square. Transaction gossiping is a similar concept where nodes share information about transactions with their peers. This helps ensure all nodes have a relatively up-to-date view of the transaction pool, facilitating efficient transaction processing across the network.

Example: Broadcasting and Gossiping with GenServer (Code Snippet):

```elixir
Elixir
defmodule MyApp.PeerNode do
 use GenServer
 def init(state) do
  {:ok, state}
 end
 def handle_cast({:broadcast_block, block}, state) do
  # Broadcast the block to other connected nodes
  send_message(other_nodes, {:new_block, block})
  {:noreply, state}
 end
 def handle_cast({:new_transaction, transaction}, state) do
  # Add the transaction to the pool and potentially gossip
to peers
```

```
  add_transaction_to_pool(transaction)
  maybe_gossip_transaction(transaction)
  {:noreply, state}
 end
 # Implementations for send_message,
add_transaction_to_pool, and
maybe_gossip_transaction omitted for brevity
end
```

This code snippet expands on the previous GenServer example (MyApp.PeerNode). The handle_cast function now showcases not only broadcasting a new block ({:broadcast_block, block}) but also handling a new transaction ({:new_transaction, transaction}). The latter might involve adding the transaction to the pool and potentially gossiping it to other connected nodes using the maybe_gossip_transaction function (implementation omitted for brevity).

The specific implementation details for these functionalities will vary depending on the chosen blockchain platform and consensus mechanism (we'll explore those in the next chapter). However, understanding these core functionalities equips you with a solid foundation for building the processing heart of your blockchain node.

Additional Considerations:

- Incentives: In some blockchains, nodes are incentivized for participating in the network (e.g., mining rewards in Proof of Work). Implementing functionalities to handle these incentives might be necessary depending on the chosen consensus mechanism.

- Error Handling: Things don't always go according to plan in the digital world. Robust error handling mechanisms are crucial for ensuring your node gracefully handles unexpected situations and maintains network stability.

By implementing these functionalities and considering additional factors, you'll transform your node from a blueprint into a powerhouse, actively participating in the maintenance and growth of the blockchain network.

4.3 Node Communication and Synchronization

Imagine a choir performance. Each singer needs to be in sync, listening to their fellow performers and adjusting their melody accordingly. Similarly, in a blockchain network, nodes need to communicate and synchronize data to maintain a consistent state. In this section, we'll explore the key mechanisms that enable this harmonious collaboration.

1. Gossip Protocols:

Gossip protocols are like a decentralized information sharing network. Nodes constantly exchange information about transactions and blocks with their peers. This helps ensure all nodes have a relatively up-to-date view of the network's state.

Benefits:

- Scalability: Gossip protocols are scalable because the communication load is distributed among all nodes. There's no central coordinator that gets overloaded as the network grows.
- Decentralization: Gossip protocols reinforce the decentralized nature of blockchains by not relying on a single source of information.

Example: Simple Gossiping Mechanism (Code Snippet):

```elixir
Elixir
defmodule MyApp.PeerNode do
 use GenServer
 def handle_cast({:new_transaction, transaction}, state) do
   # Add the transaction to the pool (already implemented)
   add_transaction_to_pool(transaction)
   # Gossip the transaction to a random subset of connected nodes
   gossip_to_random_peers(transaction)
   {:noreply, state}
 end
 defp gossip_to_random_peers(transaction) do
   Enum.each(Enum.sample(connected_nodes(), gossip_fanout), fn node ->
     GenServer.cast(node, {:new_transaction, transaction})
```

```
  end)
 end
end
```

This code snippet expands on the previous PeerNode GenServer example. The handle_cast function now includes a gossip_to_random_peers function (not shown in detail for brevity). This function selects a random subset of connected nodes (simulating gossip) and sends them a message containing the new transaction using GenServer.cast.

2. Consensus Algorithms:

Imagine a group project where everyone needs to agree on the final outcome. Consensus algorithms in blockchains serve a similar purpose. They are the rules that govern how nodes agree on the valid chain of blocks and prevent inconsistencies in the blockchain ledger.

Examples of Consensus Algorithms (with code snippets):

- Proof of Work (PoW): This is the algorithm used by Bitcoin. Miners compete to solve complex puzzles, and the winner gets to add the next block to the chain. While not shown here due to its complexity, PoW algorithms typically involve hashing techniques and verifying proof-of-work within the mined block.
- Proof of Stake (PoS): In PoS, nodes are selected to create blocks based on their stake (holdings) in the cryptocurrency. Here's a simplified example using a lottery analogy:

```elixir
Elixir
defmodule MyApp.BlockProposer do
  def propose_block(transactions) do
    # Simplified PoS logic: randomly select a node weighted
by its stake
    nodes = get_connected_nodes()
    weighted_nodes = Enum.map(nodes, fn node -> {node,
get_stake(node)} end)
    selected_node =
Enum.weighted_random(weighted_nodes)
    if selected_node do
      GenServer.cast(selected_node, {:propose_block,
transactions})
    end
  end
end
```

This simplified example showcases a BlockProposer module. The propose_block function assigns higher chances of proposing a block to nodes with a larger stake (simulated by weights in the Enum.weighted_random function). This is a basic illustration of the PoS concept, and real-world implementations involve more sophisticated selection mechanisms.

The specific consensus algorithm used depends on the chosen blockchain platform and its design goals. Each algorithm has its own advantages and disadvantages in terms of security, scalability, and energy efficiency.

3. Putting it All Together: Communication for Consensus

Communication and consensus algorithms work hand-in-hand. Nodes exchange information about transactions and blocks through gossip protocols. This information is then used by the consensus algorithm to determine which chain of blocks is the valid one.

Example: Broadcasting a New Block (Code Snippet):

```elixir
Elixir
defmodule MyApp.Miner do
  def mine_block(transactions) do
    # Create a new block with the transactions
    new_block = create_block(transactions)
    # Validate the block using the previously implemented
validator
    if validate_block(new_block) do
      # Broadcast the block to all connected nodes
      MyApp.PeerNode.broadcast_block(new_block)
    end
  end
end
```

This code snippet showcases a simplified Miner module. The mine_block function creates a new block with transactions and validates it. If valid, it utilizes the previously discussed broadcast_block function (potentially from the PeerNode module) to broadcast the new block to all connected nodes. This allows other nodes to receive the block, validate it according to the consensus algorithm, and potentially add it to their local copy of the blockchain.

The specific communication mechanisms and their integration with consensus algorithms will vary depending on the chosen blockchain platform. However, understanding these core concepts equips you with a solid foundation for comprehending how nodes collaborate to maintain a secure and consistent blockchain network.

Chapter 5: Consensus Mechanisms

In Chapter 5, We'll delve into the fascinating world of consensus mechanisms. Imagine a group project where everyone needs to agree on the "one true version" of a document. That's exactly what consensus mechanisms achieve in blockchains – ensuring all nodes agree on the valid chain of blocks and preventing inconsistencies in the ledger. We'll explore some of the most critical algorithms that power the world of decentralized networks.

5.1 Overview of Consensus Algorithms

In blockchains, ensuring everyone agrees on the truth is paramount. This is where consensus algorithms come in – they are the fundamental mechanisms that guarantee all nodes in a network concur on the valid chain of blocks. Imagine a group project where everyone needs to agree on the single source of truth for a document; consensus algorithms achieve a similar feat in a distributed and decentralized manner. Here, we'll explore some of the most prominent consensus algorithms, providing a clear understanding of their roles in blockchains:

Proof of Work (PoW):

This veteran of the blockchain world is the algorithm that powers Bitcoin. It functions like a global lottery, where miners compete by solving complex mathematical puzzles.

The victor earns the right to add the next block to the blockchain and receive some cryptocurrency as a reward. While PoW offers strong security, it can be computationally demanding and consume significant amounts of energy.

Example (Simplified):

Elixir
```elixir
defmodule MyApp.Miner do
  def mine_block(transactions) do
    # (Oversimplified) Simulate hashing difficulty by
checking if a random number is less than a target value
    cond do
      Enum.random(1..1000) < get_difficulty() ->
        # Block hash found! Create and validate the block
        block = create_block(transactions)
        if validate_block(block) do
          # Valid block, add it to the chain and claim the reward!
          # (omitted for simplicity)
        end
      end
      true ->
        # Keep mining (trying to find a valid hash)
        mine_block(transactions)
    end
  end
end
```

This is an extremely simplified example for illustrative purposes. Real-world PoW algorithms involve complex hashing techniques and verification processes to ensure security.

Proof of Stake (PoS):

As an eco-friendly alternative to PoW, Proof of Stake is gaining traction. In PoS, the selection of nodes to create new blocks is based on their stake (holdings) in the cryptocurrency. Think of it like a raffle where the more coins you hold, the higher the chance of being chosen to propose the next block. This approach significantly reduces energy consumption compared to PoW, but it might introduce different security considerations.

Example (Simplified PoS Selection):

```Elixir
defmodule MyApp.BlockProposer do
  def propose_block(transactions) do
    # Simplified PoS logic: randomly select a node weighted by its stake
    nodes = get_connected_nodes()
    weighted_nodes = Enum.map(nodes, fn node -> {node, get_stake(node)} end)
    selected_node = Enum.weighted_random(weighted_nodes)
    if selected_node do
      GenServer.cast(selected_node, {:propose_block, transactions})
    end
  end
end
```

This code snippet demonstrates a simplified BlockProposer module. The propose_block function assigns a higher chance of proposing a block to nodes with a larger stake (simulated by weights in the Enum.weighted_random function). This is a basic illustration, and real-world PoS implementations involve more sophisticated selection mechanisms.

Byzantine Fault Tolerance (BFT):

Designed for ultra-high security and fault tolerance, BFT algorithms are the heavyweights in the consensus arena. They can handle situations where some nodes might be unreliable or even malicious. However, BFT algorithms are computationally intensive, making them less suitable for all blockchain applications due to their performance implications.

These are just a few examples of the diverse consensus mechanisms available. The selection of the most suitable algorithm depends on the specific requirements of the blockchain platform, such as security, scalability, and performance needs.

Here's an additional concept to consider:
- Delegated Proof of Stake (DPoS): A variation of PoS, DPoS introduces elected delegates who validate transactions and create blocks on behalf of other stakeholders. This can improve scalability but introduces a layer of centralization compared to pure PoS.

The world of consensus algorithms is constantly evolving. New mechanisms are being developed to address the challenges and opportunities presented by blockchain technology. As you delve deeper into this field, stay curious and explore the latest advancements!

5.2 Implementing Basic Consensus in Elixir

Now that we've explored the key concepts behind consensus mechanisms, let's get hands-on and build a basic consensus module in Elixir! While this won't be a full-fledged implementation, it will showcase the core functionalities involved in reaching agreement on the validity of blocks.

Real-world consensus mechanisms are far more complex and involve sophisticated cryptographic operations and security considerations. This example serves as a stepping stone to understanding the fundamental principles.

Building the Consensus Module:
Here's a breakdown of a basic Consensus module written in Elixir:

Elixir
```elixir
defmodule MyApp.Consensus do
  # Function to validate a block's integrity
  def validate_block(block) do
    # Check if the block hash is valid based on its content
    is_valid_hash?(block.hash, block.data) &&
```

```
  # Check if the previous block hash matches the chain's
tip
  get_previous_block_hash() == block.previous_hash
  end
  # Function to simulate choosing a validator for block
creation (e.g., in PoS)
  def choose_winner(validators) do
  # (Simplified approach) Randomly select a validator
  Enum.random(validators)
  end
end
```

Explanation:
- validate_block function: This function ensures the
  block's integrity by performing two crucial checks:
  - Hash Validation: It verifies if the block's hash is
    a valid representation of its content using a
    cryptographic function (implementation of
    is_valid_hash? omitted for brevity).
  - Chain Consistency: It checks if the
    previous_hash in the block points to the
    current tip (latest block) of the chain, ensuring
    the block is being added to the correct
    sequence.
- choose_winner function: This function simulates the
  process of selecting a validator to create a new block.
  In a real-world scenario, the selection might depend
  on the chosen consensus mechanism (e.g., stake in
  PoS). Here, we've kept it simple with a random
  selection from a list of validators.

Using the Consensus Module:

Elixir

```elixir
# Get the latest block from the chain
latest_block = get_latest_block()
# Simulate receiving a new block proposal
new_block = create_block(transactions)
# Validate the new block using the consensus module
if MyApp.Consensus.validate_block(new_block) do
  # Check if the new block builds on the latest block
  if new_block.previous_hash == latest_block.hash do
    # Potential consensus logic: broadcast the block to other
nodes
    # (omitted for simplicity)
  else
    # The new block doesn't follow the chain, reject it!
  end
else
  # The new block failed validation, reject it!
end
```

This code snippet demonstrates how the Consensus module can be used in practice. It retrieves the latest block, simulates receiving a new block proposal, and then validates it using the validate_block function. If the block is valid and builds upon the existing chain, it could potentially be broadcast to other nodes for further processing (specific consensus logic omitted for brevity).

This is a highly simplified example. Real-world consensus mechanisms involve additional steps, such as:

- Disseminating block proposals: Nodes need to communicate new block proposals to other participants in the network.

- Resolving conflicts: In some cases, multiple valid block proposals might emerge simultaneously. The consensus mechanism needs to determine the canonical block (the one that gets added to the chain).
- Security measures: Robust consensus mechanisms incorporate cryptographic techniques and economic incentives to prevent malicious actors from manipulating the block creation process.

Here's an additional code examples for illustrative purposes:

1. Simulating Proof of Stake Selection (Simplified):

Elixir
```elixir
defmodule MyApp.Consensus do
  # ... (existing validate_block function)
  def choose_winner(validators) do
    # Simplified PoS logic: randomly select a validator weighted by its stake
    weighted_nodes = Enum.map(validators, fn node -> {node, get_stake(node)} end)
    Enum.weighted_random(weighted_nodes)
  end
end
```

This code snippet expands on the Consensus module, showcasing a simplified approach to choosing a validator in a Proof of Stake (PoS) scenario. The choose_winner function assigns a higher chance of being selected to nodes with a larger stake (represented by weights in the Enum.weighted_random function). This is a basic illustration, and real-world PoS implementations involve more sophisticated selection mechanisms based on factors like steak and online availability.

2. Example: Broadcasting a Validated Block (Simplified):

```elixir
Elixir
defmodule MyApp.PeerNode do
 # ... (existing functions)
 def handle_block_validation(block) do
  if MyApp.Consensus.validate_block(block) do
   # Broadcast the valid block to connected nodes
   MyApp.PeerNode.broadcast_block(block)
  end
 end
end
```

This snippet demonstrates a PeerNode module that interacts with the Consensus module. The handle_block_validation function receives a block, validates it using Consensus.validate_block, and if valid, broadcasts it to connected nodes using a broadcast_block function (not shown for brevity). This showcases how validated blocks can be propagated through the network for further processing within the chosen consensus mechanism.

These are simplified examples, and actual consensus mechanisms involve more intricate message passing, conflict resolution procedures, and security measures. However, they provide a stepping stone for understanding the core principles of agreement in blockchain networks.

By understanding these core functionalities and keeping security considerations in mind, you can grasp the essence of how consensus mechanisms power the agreement process in blockchains. As you delve deeper into this field, explore more advanced consensus mechanisms and their specific implementations in various blockchain platforms.

5.3 Ensuring Network Security and Integrity

While consensus mechanisms are the cornerstones of agreement in blockchains, security remains paramount. A secure and trustworthy network is essential for maintaining a reliable and tamper-proof ledger. Here, we'll explore some key security considerations during consensus:

- Sybil Attacks: Imagine a malicious actor trying to create a large number of fake nodes to manipulate the consensus process. This is known as a Sybil attack. Techniques like requiring a minimum stake (in PoS) or proof-of-work (in PoW) can help mitigate this risk by making it expensive to create and maintain a large number of fake identities.
- 51% Attacks: This scenario involves a single entity or group controlling more than half of the computing power (in PoW) or stake (in PoS) in the network. With this majority, they could potentially disrupt the network by manipulating block creation or

preventing valid transactions from being included. Security measures like decentralization (distributing participation across many nodes) and economic incentives (penalties for malicious behavior) can help prevent such attacks.

- Byzantine Faults: In rare cases, nodes might behave erratically or provide misleading information. These are known as Byzantine faults. While BFT algorithms are specifically designed to tolerate such faults, they come at a cost in terms of performance overhead.

Code Considerations for Security:

While we haven't focused heavily on code examples in this section (due to the focus on security principles), it's important to remember that secure coding practices are crucial when implementing consensus mechanisms. Here are some general guidelines:

- Use well-established cryptographic libraries: Don't reinvent the wheel. Leverage existing and secure cryptographic libraries for hashing and other cryptographic operations.
- Validate all inputs: Always validate data received from other nodes before using it in the consensus process. This helps prevent malicious actors from injecting invalid information.
- Implement proper error handling: Anticipate and handle potential errors gracefully to prevent the consensus process from being compromised.

Remember: Security is an ongoing battle. As new threats emerge, developers need to stay informed and adapt their implementations to address them. While we can't directly showcase code examples for malicious activities, we can illustrate security concepts through defensive measures and code comments:

1. Mitigating Sybil Attacks (Code Example):

```elixir
Elixir
defmodule MyApp.PeerNode do
  # ... (existing functions)
  def handle_new_peer(peer_info) do
    # Check if the peer already exists (prevent duplicate
registrations)
    if not connected?(peer_info) do
      # (Perform other validation checks)
      # ...
      # If validation passes, add the peer with a minimum
stake requirement (if applicable)
      if MyApp.StakeManager.get_stake(peer_info) >=
minimum_stake() do
        add_peer(peer_info)
      end
    end
  end
end
```

This code snippet (focusing on a PeerNode module) demonstrates a basic approach to mitigating Sybil attacks. It checks if a new peer is already registered before adding it. Additionally, you could implement other validation checks (commented out with "...") to assess the legitimacy of the peer. In a Proof-of-Stake (PoS) scenario, a minimum stake requirement (enforced by the MyApp.StakeManager.get_stake function and the minimum_stake function) can help prevent Sybil attacks by making it expensive to create and maintain a large number of nodes with low stake.

2. Secure Coding Practices (Code Comments):

```elixir
defmodule MyApp.Consensus do
  # ... (existing validate_block function)
  def validate_block(block) do
     # Validate block hash based on cryptographic hash function (use a well-established library)
    if Crypto.Hash.verify(block.hash, block.data) do
    # ... (other validation checks)
   end
  end
end
```

This code snippet (part of the Consensus module) highlights the importance of using well-established cryptographic libraries. The commented line suggests using a function like Crypto.Hash.verify (assuming an Elixir library like cryptoex is available) to validate the block hash. This approach leverages the security expertise built into the cryptographic library.

Here are some additional points to consider:

1. Incentive Design and Security (Example):

The economic incentives embedded within the consensus mechanism play a crucial role in encouraging honest participation. Nodes are rewarded for following the rules and penalized for malicious behavior.

Example: In Proof-of-Work (PoW) blockchains like Bitcoin, miners earn rewards for successfully mining a block. This incentivizes miners to contribute computing power to the network and discourages them from attempting to disrupt it, as such actions would jeopardize their chance of earning rewards.

Code Snippet (for illustration purposes only):

```Elixir
defmodule MyApp.Miner do
  # ... (existing mine_block function)
  def handle_block_mined(block) do
    # (Assuming successful mining)
    # Reward the miner for adding a valid block to the chain
    reward_miner(block.miner, mining_reward())
  end
end
```

While this code snippet doesn't showcase the actual mining process (which is complex), the handle_block_mined function illustrates the concept of rewarding miners for adding valid blocks. This reward structure incentivizes honest participation in securing the network.

2. Importance of Regular Audits:

Security audits by qualified professionals can help identify and address vulnerabilities in the consensus mechanism implementation. Regular audits are essential for maintaining a secure network.

Example: Imagine a scenario where a subtle bug in the consensus code allows a malicious actor to manipulate block validation in a specific way. A security audit might uncover this vulnerability before it can be exploited.

Code (not applicable): Security audits are manual processes performed by security experts. They wouldn't involve writing specific code within the consensus mechanism itself.

3. Keeping Up-to-Date:

The blockchain ecosystem is constantly evolving. New threats and vulnerabilities emerge, and new security best practices are developed. Staying informed is crucial for maintaining a secure network.

Example: A new research paper might identify a potential attack vector against a specific consensus mechanism. By keeping up with such developments, developers can implement appropriate security measures to mitigate these risks.

Code (not applicable): Staying up-to-date is an ongoing process that involves following security research, attending conferences, and collaborating with the security community.

Security is a continuous effort. By understanding these concepts, implementing robust security practices, and staying informed, developers can contribute to building secure and trustworthy blockchain networks that can withstand evolving threats.

Chapter 6: Smart Contracts with Elixir

In this chapter, we delve into the fascinating world of smart contracts – the self-executing programs that live on blockchains. Imagine a vending machine on steroids, programmed to dispense goodies based on predefined rules, all transparently recorded on a distributed ledger. That's the essence of smart contracts! Let's dive in and explore how Elixir empowers you to build these marvels.

6.1 Introduction to Smart Contracts

Smart contracts are like vending machines for the digital age. Instead of dispensing snacks based on inserted coins, they execute pre-programmed instructions on a blockchain when certain conditions are met. Imagine a rental agreement that automatically releases the security deposit when the lease is fulfilled – that's the power of smart contracts in action!

Here's a breakdown of key concepts to understand smart contracts:

- What are they? Smart contracts are self-executing programs stored on a blockchain. They can automate agreements, manage transactions, and enforce rules without the need for a central authority.

Key Characteristics:

- Immutable: The code of a smart contract cannot be changed after deployment, ensuring the terms of the agreement remain tamper-proof.
- Transparent: All transactions involving a smart contract are publicly viewable on the blockchain, fostering trust and accountability.
- Trustless: Smart contracts eliminate the need for a central intermediary, as the code itself dictates how the agreement is executed.

How do they work? Here's a simplified view:

1. Deployment: The smart contract code is written in a blockchain-compatible language (like Solidity for Ethereum) and deployed on a chosen blockchain platform.
2. Interaction: Users can interact with the smart contract by sending transactions that trigger specific functions within the code.
3. Execution: When the predefined conditions are met, the smart contract code executes automatically, updating its state on the blockchain (think of it as updating the vending machine's internal ledger).

Example:

Imagine a marketplace smart contract for buying and selling digital art. The contract might hold the artwork in escrow until the buyer pays the agreed-upon price. Once the payment is received, the contract would automatically transfer ownership of the art to the buyer. This eliminates the need for a trusted intermediary and ensures a secure transaction for both parties.

Code Example (Simplified):

Solidity

```solidity
// Example smart contract for a simple marketplace
contract ArtMarketplace {
  address payable public seller; // Address of the seller
  address payable public buyer;  // Address of the buyer
(initially empty)
  string public artTitle;     // Title of the artwork
  constructor(address payable _seller, string memory
_artTitle) public {
    seller = _seller;
    artTitle = _artTitle;
  }
  // Function for buyer to purchase the art
  function buyArt() public payable {
    require(msg.value >= price, "Insufficient payment
provided"); // Check if sent value meets the price
    buyer = msg.sender;  // Record the buyer's address
  }
  // Function for seller to withdraw funds after a sale
  function withdrawFunds() public {
    require(buyer != address(0), "Art not yet purchased"); //
Check if there's a buyer
    seller.transfer(address(this).balance); // Transfer funds
to the seller
  }
}
```

This is a very basic example for illustrative purposes. Real-world smart contracts involve security measures, error handling, and more sophisticated functionalities.

By understanding these core concepts, you're equipped to grasp the fundamental principles behind smart contracts and their potential to revolutionize how agreements are executed in a digital world.

6.2 Writing and Deploying Smart Contracts

Imagine you're constructing a self-operating vending machine on the blockchain – that's essentially what writing and deploying a smart contract entails. Here, we'll delve into the exciting process of crafting these automated agreements in Elixir, a language well-suited for building robust smart contracts.

The Building Blocks:
- Development Environment: You'll need a suitable environment to write your smart contract code. For Elixir, popular options include tools like iex (Elixir's interactive shell) or IDEs with Elixir support.
- Smart Contract Language: While various languages are used for smart contracts (like Solidity for Ethereum), we'll focus on using Elixir in this section. Elixir's focus on concurrency and fault tolerance makes it a powerful choice for building stateful and reliable smart contracts.

- GenServer Behavior: Elixir's GenServer behavior provides a solid foundation for building smart contracts. It offers features like process supervision, message handling, and state management – crucial aspects for a well-functioning smart contract.

The Development Process:
1. Contract Design: Define the functionalities and state variables your smart contract will require. Think about the actions it should allow (e.g., sending funds, storing data) and the information it needs to maintain (e.g., balances, ownership records).
2. Elixir Code Implementation: Write the smart contract code using Elixir syntax. Here's a simplified example showcasing a basic EscrowContract:

```elixir
Elixir
defmodule EscrowContract do
 use GenServer
 def init(initial_amount, sender, recipient) do
  {:ok, %{amount: initial_amount, sender: sender,
recipient: recipient}}
 end
 def handle_call(:release_funds, _from) do
  # (Simplified logic) Simulate releasing funds to the
recipient
  {:noreply, %{amount: 0}}
 end
 # ... other functions for depositing funds and checking
balance
end
```

This example demonstrates a contract that holds funds in escrow until a specific action triggers their release. The GenServer behavior is used to manage the contract's state (the held amount) and handle function calls (handle_call).

3. Deployment: Once your contract code is written, it needs to be deployed to a blockchain platform that supports smart contracts. The specific deployment process will vary depending on the chosen platform. Some platforms offer tools and APIs to facilitate this process.

Important Considerations:
- Security: Smart contract security is paramount. Even minor vulnerabilities can lead to significant financial losses. Thorough testing, code audits, and best practices are crucial for secure smart contract development.
- Real-World Complexity: While the provided examples are simplified, real-world smart contracts often involve more intricate logic, error handling, and interaction with other smart contracts or oracles (external data feeds).

Here are some more code examples to showcase different functionalities of smart contracts written in Elixir:

1. Simple Supply Chain Contract:

Elixir
```
defmodule SupplyChainContract do
  use GenServer
  def init(product_id, origin) do
```

```elixir
    {:ok, %{product_id: product_id, origin: origin, owner:
origin}}
  end
  def handle_call(:change_ownership, _from,
new_owner) do
    {:ok, %{owner: new_owner}}
  end
  def handle_call(:get_owner, _from) do
    {:reply, {:ok, owner}, state}
  end
end
```

This example demonstrates a basic supply chain contract that tracks product ownership. It allows changing ownership (through the change_ownership function) and retrieving the current owner (get_owner). This is a simplified illustration, and real-world supply chain contracts might involve additional functionalities like recording timestamps and locations.

   2. Multi-Signature Wallet Contract:

```elixir
Elixir
defmodule MultiSigWallet do
  use GenServer
  def init(minimum_signatures, authorized_keys) do
    {:ok, %{minimum_signatures: minimum_signatures,
authorized_keys: authorized_keys, transactions: []}}
  end
  def handle_call({:submit_transaction, tx_data}, from)
do
```

```
  # Check if sender is authorized and update transaction
list
  {:noreply, update_state(tx_data, from)}
 end
 def handle_call(:execute_transactions, _from) do
  # (Simplified logic) Simulate executing transactions if
enough signatures are collected
  # ...
 end
 # ... helper functions for signature verification and state
updates
end
```

This example showcases a multi-signature wallet contract. It requires a minimum number of approvals (minimum_signatures) from a set of authorized parties (authorized_keys) before a transaction can be executed (execute_transactions). This can be useful for scenarios requiring shared control over funds.

Remember, These are just snippets for illustrative purposes. Real-world smart contract development involves security considerations, error handling, and adherence to specific blockchain platforms' functionalities. As you explore further, you'll encounter more complex examples and best practices for building secure and robust smart contracts with Elixir.

6.3 Interacting with Smart Contracts

Imagine a vending machine where you can't just insert coins — you need to send a specific instruction to dispense your desired snack. That's similar to how you interact with smart contracts on a blockchain. In this section, we'll explore how to call the functions defined within your smart contract and retrieve the responses.

Here's a breakdown of the key concepts:

- Transactions: These are messages sent to the blockchain network that trigger actions. When interacting with a smart contract, you construct a transaction specifying the smart contract's address and the function you want to call (like selecting a product in the vending machine).
- Function Calls: Smart contracts define functions that encapsulate specific actions. By sending a transaction with the appropriate function name and any required data (like the amount to withdraw), you initiate the execution of that function within the smart contract.
- Events: Smart contracts can emit events after a function executes. These events provide information about the state changes that occurred within the contract. Your application can listen for these events to understand the outcome of the interaction.

Here's how the interaction happens:

1. Transaction Construction: You create a transaction using tools provided by the blockchain platform or

your development environment. This transaction specifies:

- ○ The target smart contract address
- ○ The function you want to call (e.g., withdraw in our example)
- ○ Any required data for the function (e.g., the amount to withdraw)
- ○ (Optional) Additional fees to cover the transaction cost on the blockchain network

2. Transaction Broadcast: The constructed transaction is broadcast to the blockchain network. Miners or validators on the network pick it up and process it according to the platform's consensus mechanism.

3. Smart Contract Execution: Once the transaction is validated, the corresponding function within the smart contract is executed. The contract's state might be updated based on the function's logic.

4. Event Emission (Optional): The smart contract might emit an event after successful function execution. This event contains details about the changes that occurred (e.g., the new balance after a withdrawal).

5. Response and Event Handling: Your application can listen for the transaction's completion and any emitted events. This allows you to react to the outcome of the interaction with the smart contract.

Code Example (Simplified)

Elixir
```
# Assuming a function `withdraw(amount)` exists in the
smart contract
transaction = %{
```

```
  to: smart_contract_address,  # Address of the smart
contract
  value: 0,              # No value sent for this call (optional)
  data: {:withdraw, 100}      # Data for the withdraw
function (amount)
}
# Broadcast the transaction to the blockchain
broadcast(transaction)
# Listen for the transaction confirmation and any emitted
events
receive do
  {:transaction_confirmed, tx_hash} ->
    # Handle successful transaction
  {:event, event_name, data} ->
    # Handle emitted event (optional)
end
```

Here are some more examples to showcase interacting with different functionalities of smart contracts:

1. Voting on a Decentralized Application (dApp):

Imagine a dApp where users can vote on proposals. Here's a simplified code snippet (assuming an Elixir library for interacting with the blockchain):

```
Elixir
# Connect to the blockchain node
library.connect(blockchain_url)
# Get the voting contract address
voting_contract_address =
get_contract_address(:VotingContract)
```

```elixir
# Construct a transaction to vote for proposal_id 1
transaction = library.build_transaction(
  to: voting_contract_address,
  data: {:vote, 1}  # Data for the vote function (proposal ID)
)
# Sign the transaction (assuming user has a crypto wallet)
signed_transaction = sign_transaction(transaction)
# Broadcast the signed transaction
library.broadcast_transaction(signed_transaction)
# Listen for the transaction confirmation
receive do
  {:transaction_confirmed, tx_hash} ->
    # Inform the user that their vote was cast successfully
end
```

2. Calling a Contract Function to Get Data:

Imagine a smart contract that stores product information. Here's how you might retrieve it:

Elixir
```elixir
# Connect and get the contract address (same as previous example)
# Construct a transaction to call the `get_product_name` function
transaction = library.build_transaction(
  to: voting_contract_address,
  data: {:get_product_name, product_id}  # Data for the function (product ID)
)
# Broadcast the transaction and wait for confirmation
```

```
# After confirmation, the contract might emit an event
with the product name
receive do
  {:event, "ProductName", product_name} ->
  # Display the retrieved product name to the user
end
```

These are just snippets for illustrative purposes. Real-world interaction involves security considerations like proper user authentication and authorization, error handling, and using libraries or tools specific to the chosen blockchain platform. By understanding these core concepts, you're equipped to interact with smart contracts and leverage their power to automate agreements and execute code on the blockchain in a programmatic way.

Chapter 7: Optimizing Performance

In Chapter 7, We'll discuss performance optimization. Just like a well-tuned race car, an optimized Elixir application can handle heavy workloads with speed and efficiency. Here, we'll explore techniques to keep your applications running smoothly, scaling them to meet growing demands, and ensuring they stay responsive under pressure.

7.1 Techniques for Improving Performance

Imagine a bustling marketplace application. To keep things running smoothly under heavy traffic, performance optimization is crucial. Luckily, Elixir offers several built-in advantages and techniques to ensure your application stays speedy and responsive. Here, we'll explore some key approaches to enhance your Elixir application's performance:

1. Concurrency:

Elixir excels in handling concurrency, meaning it can manage multiple tasks simultaneously. This is a significant advantage for web applications that often juggle multiple user requests. Here's how it works:
- Processes and Tasks: Elixir utilizes lightweight processes (GenServers) and short-lived tasks (Task)

for concurrent execution. Think of them as mini-programs running alongside your main application, each handling a specific request or computation.

- Benefits: By leveraging concurrency, your application can process multiple requests at once, improving responsiveness and user experience. Imagine searching for products in the marketplace – while one user's search is ongoing, another user's request to view a product detail page can be processed concurrently.

Code Example (Simplified):

Elixir
```
def search_products(query) do
  Task.spawn(fn -> search_category(query, :electronics)
end)
  Task.spawn(fn -> search_category(query, :clothing)
end)
  # ... (Process other parts of the request while searches run
concurrently)
  # Combine and return results from both searches
end
```

This simplified example demonstrates spawning two tasks to search for products in different categories concurrently. While these tasks are running, the main process can focus on other aspects of handling the user's request.

2. Distribution:

For truly large-scale applications, consider distributed computing. This involves spreading your application across multiple machines, leveraging their combined processing power. Here's how it helps:

- Horizontal Scaling: Instead of relying on a single server, you can distribute the workload across multiple servers. This allows you to handle a significant increase in traffic by adding more machines as needed.

Imagine a massive warehouse with a single entrance and exit. Distributing your application is like adding more entrances and exits, allowing for faster movement of goods (requests) within the warehouse.

3. Efficient Data Structures

The way you structure your data plays a crucial role in performance. Elixir offers efficient data structures that can significantly speed up your application:

- Maps and Keyword Lists: Use these data structures for fast lookups and key-based access. They excel at retrieving specific data points quickly, making them ideal for scenarios like retrieving product information based on an ID in your marketplace application.
- Avoiding Unnecessary Copies: When working with large datasets, be mindful of copying data unnecessarily. Techniques like referencing existing data structures can improve performance.

Choosing the right data structure for your specific use case is essential. Refer to Elixir documentation and best practices for guidance on selecting the most efficient options. Here are some more examples to showcase different techniques for improving performance in Elixir applications:

1. Utilizing GenServers for Concurrent Tasks:

Imagine a social media application where users can follow each other and see updates from their feeds. Here's how concurrency with GenServers can be beneficial:

```Elixir
defmodule UserFeed do
  use GenServer
  def init(user_id) do
    {:ok, user_id, %{posts: []}}
  end
  def handle_call(:get_feed, _from) do
    # (Simplified logic) Simulate fetching posts from
followed users concurrently
    posts = Task.async_stream(fn ->
fetch_posts_from_user(user_id) end)
    {:reply, {:ok, Enum.concat(posts)}, state}
  end
  # ... other functions for handling updates and managing
the feed
end
```

This example showcases a simplified UserFeed GenServer. The get_feed function utilizes Task.async_stream to concurrently fetch posts from users the current user follows. This approach can improve the perceived performance for the user while the posts are being retrieved.

2. Leveraging Keyword Lists for Fast Lookups:
Imagine a product catalog with various attributes like category, brand, and price. Here's how keyword lists can be used for efficient retrieval:

```elixir
Elixir
product = %{
  id: 1,
  name: "Cool Gadget",
  category: :electronics,
  brand: "MegaCorp",
  price: 100
}
# Fast lookup by category using keyword
category_lookup = Keyword.get(product, :category)  #
Returns :electronics
# Efficient price check using keyword with default value
is_affordable = Keyword.get(product, :price, 150) <= 120
# Returns true
```

This example demonstrates how keyword lists within a product map allow for quick lookups based on specific keys. This can significantly improve performance compared to iterating through the entire map structure.

By mastering these core techniques, you can significantly enhance your Elixir application's performance. In the next section, we'll delve into scalability solutions for handling even larger workloads.

7.2 Scalability Solutions

Imagine your once-quiet marketplace application has exploded in popularity! Now you're facing a happy challenge – handling a massive influx of users and transactions. This is where scalability solutions come into play. They help your application grow gracefully, maintaining performance even under increased load. Here, we'll explore two key techniques for scaling Elixir applications:

Sharding: Dividing and Conquering Data

Think of sharding as splitting a massive crowd into smaller, more manageable groups. In the context of databases, sharding involves dividing your data into smaller chunks and distributing them across multiple servers. Here's how it benefits scalability:

- Distributed Workload: By storing data on multiple servers, the overall load is distributed. This means each server handles a smaller portion of the data, improving query performance and reducing bottlenecks that might occur with a single, overloaded database.
- Horizontal Scaling: As your application grows, you can easily add more servers to the sharded cluster.

This allows you to scale horizontally, adding processing power without needing to upgrade existing hardware on a single server.

Imagine a library with a single, massive card catalog. Sharding is like dividing the catalog into smaller sections by genre (e.g., fiction, non-fiction) and placing them in separate rooms. This allows multiple librarians to assist patrons searching for books simultaneously.

Off-chain Storage: Streamlining Blockchain Interaction

While blockchains offer security and transparency, constantly interacting with them can impact performance. Off-chain storage provides a solution for data that doesn't require the full power of the blockchain. Here's how it helps:

- Reduced On-chain Load: By storing frequently accessed or less critical data (like product images in our marketplace example) off-chain in dedicated databases, you reduce the load on the blockchain itself. This frees up blockchain resources for more critical tasks that require its tamper-proof nature.
- Faster Access: Data stored off-chain can be accessed much faster than data on the blockchain. This can significantly improve the responsiveness of your application, especially for data that users frequently interact with.

Imagine a busy restaurant with a large menu. Off-chain storage is like having a separate menu board displaying popular dishes that change frequently. This allows servers to quickly take orders for these items without needing to consult the full, extensive menu book every time.

When choosing data to store off-chain, consider the trade-off between accessibility and the security guarantees offered by the blockchain. Here are some additional examples to showcase scalability solutions in action:

1. Sharding a User Table in a Distributed Marketplace: Imagine a massive user table in your marketplace application. Sharding can be implemented to distribute the load:

```
# Shard key based on user ID (simplified example)
def shard_key(user_id) do
  user_id // 1000  # Shard based on the first 3 digits of the user ID
end
# User lookup considering shard key
def get_user(user_id) do
  shard_server = get_shard_server(shard_key(user_id))
  shard_server.get_user(user_id)
end
```

In this example, the shard_key function distributes users across different servers (potentially implemented as separate Elixir nodes) based on a hashing logic (here, using the first 3 digits of the user ID). The get_user function retrieves the user information by routing the request to the appropriate shard server responsible for that user's data.

2. Off-chain Storage for Product Images: Consider storing product images in a dedicated image storage service like Amazon S3:

Elixir

```elixir
# Simplified function to upload product image off-chain
def upload_product_image(image_data, filename) do
  # Interact with image storage service API to upload the
image
  # ...
end
# Product schema with reference to off-chain image
location
product_schema = %{
  id: 1,
  name: "Cool Gadget",
  # ... other product details
  image_url: get_image_url(product_id)  # Function to
construct image URL from off-chain storage
}
```

This example showcases storing the image data off-chain in a service like S3. The product schema itself might only contain a reference to the image URL, allowing the application to retrieve the image from the off-chain storage when needed.

By understanding and implementing these scalability solutions, you can ensure your Elixir application can handle even the most demanding workloads. Remember, scalability is an ongoing process. As your application evolves, you might need to adapt your approach and explore additional techniques for optimal performance.

7.3 Monitoring and Optimizing Elixir Applications

Just like a car needs regular checkups and maintenance, your Elixir application benefits from monitoring and optimization. By proactively identifying performance bottlenecks and inefficiencies, you can ensure your application stays responsive and efficient as it grows. Here, we'll explore key techniques for keeping your Elixir applications in top shape:

Profiling Tools:

Imagine a mechanic using diagnostic tools to pinpoint issues in a car. Profiling tools serve a similar purpose for your Elixir application. They help you identify areas that are slowing down your application's performance. Here are some popular options:

- cprof: This built-in profiling tool provides detailed information about function call times and memory usage. It helps you identify functions that take an excessively long time to execute or consume a large amount of memory.
- httpoison: This library offers profiling capabilities specifically for HTTP requests. It can pinpoint slow external API calls or inefficiencies in your application's handling of HTTP requests.

How it Works:
You run your application with the profiling tool enabled. The tool collects data about how your application executes,

then presents it in a report. This report highlights areas that might require optimization.

Code Example (Using cprof):

```elixir
# Run your application with profiling enabled
cprof_result = :cprof.start(fun -> MyApp.start() end)
# After some application usage, stop profiling and analyze the results
:cprof.stop()
{:prof, _, _, profile_data} = cprof_result
# Analyze profile_data to identify performance bottlenecks
IO.puts("Functions with the most wallclock time:")
profile_data[:functions_by_wallclock] |> Enum.take(5)
|> Enum.each(fn { {name, _, _, time}, _ ->
  IO.puts("#{name}: #{time} seconds")
end)
```

Targeted Optimization:

Once you've identified performance bottlenecks through profiling, it's time to take action. Here's how to approach optimization:

- Focus on Bottlenecks: Don't try to optimize everything at once. Prioritize the functions or areas identified as the most significant performance drains in your profiling report.
- Code Restructuring: Sometimes, refactoring code or using more efficient algorithms can significantly improve performance. This might involve techniques

like memoization (caching function results) or utilizing built-in Elixir functions with better performance characteristics.

- Leveraging Concurrency: As we explored earlier, Elixir excels at concurrency. If applicable, consider restructuring your code to utilize Task or GenServer to handle tasks concurrently, potentially improving responsiveness.

Here are some more examples to showcase monitoring and optimization techniques in action:

1. Identifying Slow Database Queries with httpoison Profiling:

Imagine an e-commerce application where product listings load slowly. Profiling with httpoison can help pinpoint the culprit:

Elixir
```
# Enable profiling for HTTP requests
HTTPoison.profile(:enabled, true)
# Simulate user browsing product categories (code for browsing omitted)
# After some user interaction, analyze profiling data
profile_data = HTTPoison.profile(:data)
# Look for slow API calls to the product service
slow_calls = profile_data[:external_requests] |>
Enum.sort_by(& &1[:duration], :desc) |> Enum.take(3)
slow_calls |> Enum.each(fn { %{method: method, url: url, duration: duration}, _ ->
  IO.puts("Slow API call: #{method} #{url} - Took #{duration} ms")
```

end)

In this example, profiling with httpoison reveals potentially slow API calls to the product service. This information can guide further investigation into the database queries executed by the product service, helping identify and optimize inefficient queries that might be causing the slow product listings.

2. Optimizing a Function Using Memoization:
Imagine a function that calculates a complex mathematical formula. Profiling might reveal it's being called frequently with the same arguments. Here's how memoization can help:

```elixir
Elixir
defmodule MathUtils do
  @memo ||= %{}
  def slow_calculation(x, y) do
    # Simulate a complex calculation
    Process.sleep(100)
    x * y + Math.sin(x)
  end
  def memoized_calculation(x, y) do
    key = {x, y}
    @memo[key] |||= slow_calculation(x, y)
  end
end
```

This example introduces a memoized_calculation function that utilizes a process dictionary (@memo) to cache the results of the slow_calculation function based on the input arguments. Subsequent calls with the same arguments retrieve the cached value instead of re-executing the slow calculation, potentially improving performance.

Additional Tips:
- Stay Updated: The Elixir ecosystem is constantly evolving. Keep yourself updated on new libraries and tools that can help with performance optimization.
- Community Resources: The Elixir community is a valuable resource. Don't hesitate to seek advice and share your experiences with fellow Elixir developers.

By following these guidelines and embracing a proactive approach to monitoring and optimization, you can ensure your Elixir applications deliver exceptional performance for your users, even as your user base and application complexity grow.

Chapter 8: Security Best Practices for Elixir Applications

In this chapter, we'll delve into the exciting world of application security. Just like a well-guarded castle, your Elixir applications need robust defenses to protect user data and functionality from malicious attacks. Here, we'll explore common security threats, equip you with cryptographic tools, and guide you on establishing secure communication channels. Let's build a fortress of security for your applications!

8.1 Common Security Threats

Just like any valuable asset, your Elixir applications need protection from security threats. These threats can come in various forms, aiming to steal data, disrupt functionality, or gain unauthorized access. By understanding these common threats, you can proactively secure your applications and safeguard user information.
Here's a breakdown of key concepts:

Vulnerabilities:

These are weaknesses in your code, libraries, or system configuration that attackers can exploit. Imagine a vulnerability as a weak spot in your castle's defenses – a loose brick in the wall or a forgotten gate key.

Examples: Unvalidated user input (allowing attackers to inject malicious code), outdated libraries with known security flaws, insecure storage of sensitive data (like passwords).

Attacks:

Once attackers identify a vulnerability, they might launch an attack to compromise your system. This could involve various techniques, depending on the attacker's goals.
Examples: SQL injection attacks (manipulating database queries to steal data), Denial-of-Service attacks (flooding your application with traffic to render it unusable), Cross-Site Scripting (XSS) attacks (injecting malicious scripts into web pages).

Exploits:

These are specific methods attackers use to take advantage of vulnerabilities. Think of them as the tools in an attacker's arsenal – they leverage exploits to bypass security controls and gain unauthorized access.
Example: An attacker might discover a specific vulnerability in a commonly used library. They then develop an exploit that targets that specific vulnerability, allowing them to potentially compromise applications that use the vulnerable library.

Here's why understanding these threats is crucial:

By being aware of common vulnerabilities and attack techniques, you can take steps to mitigate risks. This proactive approach involves secure coding practices, keeping software libraries updated, and implementing robust security measures within your application.

Here are some examples to showcase different types of security threats and vulnerabilities in Elixir applications:

1.Unvalidated User Input (Vulnerability):

```elixir
Elixir
def sign_up(username, password) do
  # ... (logic to create a new user)
  "User #{username} created successfully!"
end
# Attacker can potentially inject malicious code by entering a specially crafted username
attacker_username = "evil_user<script>alert('XSS Attack!')</script>"
sign_up(attacker_username, "any_password")
```

In this example, the sign_up function doesn't validate the user-provided username. An attacker can inject malicious script into the username field, potentially leading to an XSS attack if the code is not properly sanitized before processing.

2. SQL Injection Attack (Exploiting a Vulnerability):
Imagine a login functionality where a user enters their username and password. An attacker might attempt an SQL injection attack to bypass authentication:

Elixir

```
def login(username, password) do
  query = "SELECT * FROM users WHERE username =
'#{username}' AND password = '#{password}'"
  # ... (execute query and authenticate user)
end
# Attacker can potentially bypass authentication with a
crafted username
attacker_username = "' OR '1' = '1"  # This tricks the query
to always return a row
login(attacker_username, "any_password")
```

This simplified example demonstrates a vulnerable login function. By injecting a specially crafted username that manipulates the underlying SQL query, an attacker might bypass authentication altogether. Proper input validation and using parameterized queries can help mitigate this type of vulnerability.

3. Insecure Storage of Sensitive Data (Vulnerability):
Imagine storing user passwords directly in the database without any encryption. This creates a vulnerability if an attacker gains access to the database:

Elixir
```
def create_user(username, password) do
  # ... (logic to create a new user)
  # Password stored directly in the database (insecure!)
  insert(%User{username: username, password:
password}, :users)
end
```

This example showcases insecure storage of passwords. Instead, passwords should always be hashed using a strong hashing algorithm (like Argon2) before storing them in the database. Hashing makes the passwords unreadable even if an attacker gains access to the database.

4. Denial-of-Service Attack (Attack):
An attacker might attempt a Denial-of-Service (DoS) attack to overwhelm your application with traffic, preventing legitimate users from accessing it. This attack itself doesn't exploit a vulnerability but aims to disrupt service.

Remember: These are simplified examples for illustration purposes. Real-world security threats and vulnerabilities can be more complex. Security is an ongoing process. Staying informed about new threats, adopting secure coding practices, and regularly reviewing your application's security posture are essential for building and maintaining a strong defense.

8.2 Implementing Cryptographic Functions

In the world of digital security, cryptography plays a vital role. It's like a toolbox filled with specialized instruments for safeguarding information within your Elixir applications. Let's explore some key cryptographic functions that can significantly enhance your application's security posture:

Hashing:

Imagine a unique fingerprint for data. That's essentially what hashing functions do. They take an arbitrary input (like a password or a file) and generate a fixed-size output string called a hash. This hash acts like a digital fingerprint, uniquely identifying the original data. Here are some key points about hashing:

- One-way Function: A crucial aspect of hashing is its one-way nature. It's easy to generate a hash from data, but computationally infeasible to recreate the original data from the hash alone. Think of it as a one-way street – you can walk down the street (create a hash), but it's nearly impossible to walk back up the street (recover the original data) just by looking at the destination (the hash).
- Verifying Integrity: Hashes are excellent for verifying data integrity. If the original data is modified even slightly, the generated hash will be entirely different. This allows you to detect any tampering with the data during transmission or storage. Imagine a document with a tamper-evident seal – any alteration breaks the seal, revealing data modification.

Common Hashing Algorithms:
Popular hashing algorithms used in Elixir include :crypto.hash(:sha256) and :crypto.hash(:sha512). These algorithms generate unique 256-bit and 512-bit hash values, respectively.

Code Example (Hashing a Password):

Elixir
def hash_password(password) do

```
  # Generate a secure random salt (additional layer of
security)
  salt = :crypto.strong_random_bytes(16)
  # Combine password with salt and hash using a strong
algorithm
  hashed_password = :crypto.hash(:sha256,
<<salt::binary, password::binary>>)
  # Store both the salt and the hashed password securely
  {salt, hashed_password}
end
```

This example demonstrates hashing a password. A random salt is generated to add an extra layer of security. The password and salt are then combined before hashing, making it even more challenging for attackers to crack the password even if they steal the hashed value.

Signing:

Imagine a digital signature, like the king's seal on a royal decree. In cryptography, signing allows you to verify the authenticity and origin of data. Here's how it works:

- Public-Key Cryptography: Signing utilizes public-key cryptography. This involves a key pair: a private key for signing and a public key for verification. Think of it as a two-part lock – only the private key (like a unique key) can create a signature that the public key (like the lock itself) can verify.
- Verifying Origin and Authenticity: When you sign data with your private key, the recipient can use your public key to verify the signature. This verification ensures that the data originated from you (because

only you have the private key) and hasn't been tampered with since it was signed.

Digital Signature Algorithms:
Popular signing algorithms in Elixir include EdDSA and ECDSA. These algorithms allow you to create and verify digital signatures for data integrity and authenticity.

Code Example (Simplified Signing Example):

```Elixir
# (Imagine a library for public-key cryptography)
# Generate a key pair (private_key and public_key)
{private_key, public_key} = generate_key_pair()
# Sign a message with the private key
message = "This is a signed message!"
signed_message = sign(private_key, message)
# Verify the signature using the public key
verify(public_key, signed_message, message)  # This should return true
```

This is a simplified example. Real-world implementations involve proper key management and cryptographic libraries for secure signing and verification procedures.

Encryption:

Imagine a treasure chest secured with a complex lock. Encryption scrambles data using a secret key, making it unreadable to anyone without the key. Here's what you need to understand about encryption:

- Symmetric vs. Asymmetric Encryption: There are two main types of encryption: symmetric and asymmetric. Symmetric encryption uses a single secret key for both encryption and decryption. Asymmetric encryption, as seen in signing, utilizes a public-key/private-key pair.

Use Cases for Encryption:

Encryption is often used for:
- Securing Data at Rest: Sensitive data like user passwords or financial information should be encrypted when stored at rest (e.g., in databases). Even if an attacker gains access to the storage, the encrypted data remains unreadable without the decryption key.
- Securing Data in Transit: When transmitting data over a network (like sending credit card information online), encryption protects it from eavesdropping. Imagine sending a confidential message in a sealed envelope – only the intended recipient can open it.

Encryption Algorithms:
Popular encryption algorithms in Elixir include :crypto.exap(), which is a high-performance implementation of the Advanced Encryption Standard (AES).

Code Example (Simplified Encryption Example):

Elixir
 # (Imagine a library for encryption)

```
# Secret key for encryption/decryption (keep this secure!)
secret_key = "your_secret_key_here"
# Message to be encrypted
message = "This is a confidential message!"
# Encrypt the message using the secret key
encrypted_message = encrypt(secret_key, message)
# Decrypt the message using the same secret key
decrypted_message = decrypt(secret_key,
encrypted_message)  # This should return the original
message
```

By understanding and implementing these cryptographic functions effectively, you can significantly enhance the security posture of your Elixir applications and protect sensitive data from unauthorized access or modification.

8.3 Ensuring Secure Communication

In the digital world, communication between your application and users needs to be secure. Just like a well-fortified castle protects its inhabitants, secure communication channels safeguard data as it travels between your application and the outside world. Here's how to establish robust defenses:

Secure Channels:

Imagine a fortified bridge across a moat – that's what secure channels aim to achieve. They encrypt data transmission, making it unreadable to anyone who might try to intercept it. Here's what you need to know:

- HTTPS: The most common secure channel protocol is HTTPS (Hypertext Transfer Protocol Secure). It utilizes Secure Sockets Layer (SSL) or its successor, Transport Layer Security (TLS), to encrypt communication between a web browser and a web server.
- Importance of HTTPS: When users interact with your application (e.g., logging in, submitting forms), sensitive information might be transmitted. HTTPS ensures this data remains confidential, even if someone tries to eavesdrop on the network traffic.
- Implementing HTTPS: Implementing HTTPS in Elixir applications is relatively straightforward. Popular web frameworks like Phoenix and Plug provide modules and configurations to enable HTTPS functionality.

Code Example (Enabling HTTPS with Phoenix):

Elixir

```
defmodule MyApp.Endpoint do
  use Phoenix.Endpoint, otp_app: :my_app
  # ... other endpoint configuration
  socket "/socket", MyApp.UserSocket
  # Configure HTTPS with a valid SSL certificate and key
  plug Plug.SSL,
    {:only, ["http://localhost:4000"]},
    {:keyfile, "path/to/your/server.key"},
    {:certfile, "path/to/your/server.pem"}
end
```

Access Control:

Imagine having guards at the castle gates who verify the identity and access rights of anyone entering. Access control serves a similar purpose in secure communication.

- Authentication: This process verifies a user's identity. Common techniques include username/password logins, token-based authentication, or social logins. Only authenticated users should be granted access to sensitive functionalities or data.
- Authorization: Even after authentication, users might have different levels of access within the application. Authorization determines what specific actions a user is allowed to perform. For example, a regular user might only be able to view their profile information, while an administrator might have access to modify user data.
- Implementing Access Control: Elixir frameworks like Phoenix offer built-in functionalities for user authentication and authorization. You can define access rules based on user roles and permissions, restricting unauthorized access to sensitive resources.

Secure Coding Practices

Secure coding practices are essential for building a strong foundation for secure communication. Here are some key points:

- Input Validation: Always validate user input to prevent malicious code injection or other attacks. Sanitize any data received from external sources before processing it within your application.
- Session Management: Implement secure session management techniques to prevent unauthorized access or session hijacking. Consider using techniques like session tokens with expiration times and secure storage mechanisms.
- Regular Updates: Keep your Elixir framework, libraries, and dependencies updated to benefit from security patches and address any known vulnerabilities.

Additional Examples and Code Illustrations for Ensuring Secure Communication

1. Authorization with Phoenix Guardian:
Imagine an e-commerce application where only authenticated users can view their order history. Here's a simplified example using Phoenix Guardian for authorization:

```
Elixir
defmodule MyApp.Web.Plugs.AuthorizeUser do
 import Phoenix.Controller
 def init(opts), do: opts
 def call(conn, opts) do
  user = Guardian.Plug.current_resource(conn)
  if user do
   conn
  else
```

```elixir
    conn |> put_flash(:error, "You need to be logged in to
access this page")
      ||> redirect(to: Routes.user_session_path(conn,
:new))
      ||> halt()
  end
 end
end
# In your controller function for viewing order history
defmodule MyApp.Web.OrdersController do
 use MyApp.Web, :controller
 plug MyApp.Web.Plugs.AuthorizeUser
 def index(conn, _params) do
  current_user = Guardian.Plug.current_resource(conn)
  orders = Repo.all(from o in Order, where: o.user_id ==
current_user.id)
  render(conn, "index.html", orders: orders)
 end
end
```

This example demonstrates using Phoenix.Guardian.Plug.current_resource to check if a user is authenticated before proceeding with the request. If not authorized, the user is redirected to the login page.

2. Secure Session Management with Phoenix Plug.Session: Imagine implementing a secure login system where user sessions are protected from unauthorized access:

Elixir
```elixir
defmodule MyApp.Web.Plugs.EnsureValidSession do
 import Phoenix.Controller
```

```elixir
  def init(opts), do: opts
  def call(conn, opts) do
    if conn.assigns[:current_user] do
      conn
    else
      conn |> redirect(to: Routes.user_session_path(conn,
:new))
        ||> halt()
    end
  end
end
# In your controller function after successful user login
defmodule MyApp.Web.UserController do
  use MyApp.Web, :controller
    def create(conn, %{"user" => user_params}) do
    # ... (logic to authenticate user)
    user = Repo.get_by!(User, email:
user_params["email"])
    conn |> put_session(:current_user_id, user.id)
        ||> redirect(to: Routes.home_path(conn))
    end
  end
end
```

This example showcases using Phoenix.Plug.Session to store the authenticated user's ID in the session after a successful login. The EnsureValidSession plug ensures a valid user is associated with the session before proceeding with requests requiring authentication.

Remember: Securing communication is an ongoing process. By employing these strategies and staying vigilant about security best practices, you can create a robust defense mechanism for your Elixir applications, safeguarding user data and protecting your application from unauthorized access.

Chapter 9: Case study: Building a Cryptocurrency with Elixir

This chapter takes you on a thrilling adventure – building your own cryptocurrency with Elixir! We'll explore the core components, navigate security challenges, and unleash the power of Elixir for crafting a secure and innovative digital currency.

9.1 Creating a Cryptocurrency with Elixir

The world of cryptocurrencies is fascinating, and with Elixir's capabilities, you can embark on a journey to create your own! In this section, we'll explore the fundamental building blocks of a cryptocurrency, focusing on designing the currency unit and understanding transactions.

1. Designing the Currency Unit:
Imagine a new digital asset – your very own cryptocurrency! Let's call it DigiCoin. Just like traditional currencies have units (dollars, euros), a DigiCoin represents the basic unit of value in your cryptocurrency system.

2. Transactions:
The lifeblood of any cryptocurrency is transactions. These are transfers of DigiCoins between users. When a user sends DigiCoins to another user, a transaction is created that records this exchange.

Here's what a transaction typically involves:
- Sender: The user who is sending the DigiCoins.
- Receiver: The user who is receiving the DigiCoins.
- Amount: The number of DigiCoins being transferred.
- Timestamp: The date and time the transaction occurred.

3. Transactions in Elixir:

Let's solidify these concepts with some Elixir code, keeping things simple for illustration purposes. We'll define a DigiCoin struct to represent our currency unit and a create_transaction function to create new transactions:

```elixir
Elixir
defmodule DigiCoin do
  defstruct [:amount, :sender, :receiver, :timestamp]
end
def create_transaction(sender, receiver, amount) do
  # Perform validation checks (explained later)
  # ...
  # If validation passes, create a new DigiCoin transaction
  %DigiCoin{amount: amount, sender: sender, receiver: receiver, timestamp: DateTime.utc_now()}
end
```

Explanation:
- The DigiCoin struct defines the fields associated with a DigiCoin transaction:
  - amount: The number of DigiCoins being transferred.
  - sender: The user sending the DigiCoins.
  - receiver: The user receiving the DigiCoins.

- o timestamp: The date and time the transaction occurred.
- The create_transaction function takes three arguments: sender, receiver, and amount.
- Inside the function (represented by the ... placeholder), we would typically perform various validation checks before creating the transaction. This might involve ensuring the sender has sufficient funds and verifying the transaction follows the defined rules of your cryptocurrency.
- If the validation checks pass, the function creates a new DigiCoin struct with the provided information and the current timestamp.

TThis is a simplified example. Real-world cryptocurrencies involve complex cryptography, digital signatures, and a secure distributed ledger system to manage transactions securely. However, it provides a foundational understanding for building upon.

4. Transaction Validation:
Before finalizing a transaction, it's crucial to validate it. This helps prevent fraudulent activities like:
- Double-Spending: A user trying to spend the same DigiCoins twice.
- Insufficient Funds: A user attempting to send more DigiCoins than they actually own.

Transaction validation mechanisms can vary depending on the chosen approach for your cryptocurrency. It's a critical aspect to explore further as you delve deeper into cryptocurrency development.

In conclusion, this section provided a foundational understanding of designing a currency unit and creating transactions in your Elixir-based cryptocurrency. Remember, this is just the beginning! As you explore further, you'll encounter exciting challenges and delve into the fascinating world of blockchain technology to build a secure and robust cryptocurrency system.

9.2 Managing Wallets and Transactions

In the dynamic world of cryptocurrencies, secure wallets and reliable transaction management form the backbone of any system. This section delves deeper into these crucial aspects, taking our understanding of DigiCoin to the next level.

Secure Wallets

Imagine a digital fortress safeguarding your valuable DigiCoins. User wallets play this vital role, allowing users to hold, manage, and interact with their cryptocurrency holdings. Here's a breakdown of the key concepts that empower secure wallets:

- Private Keys:

Private keys are the cornerstone of security in a cryptocurrency system. These cryptographically generated keys act like passwords specifically designed for accessing your wallet. They hold immense power – they are used to sign transactions, proving ownership of the DigiCoins you're sending. Crucially, never share your private key with anyone! Keeping it confidential is paramount for maintaining control over your DigiCoins.

- Public Keys:

Public keys are mathematically derived from private keys and serve a distinct purpose. Unlike private keys, they are intended to be shared publicly. Imagine them as a publicly viewable address for your DigiCoin holdings. Anyone can use your public key to verify the authenticity of transactions signed with your corresponding private key. This transparency fosters trust within the network.

Conceptualizing Wallets:

A user's wallet typically stores essential information:
- Balance: This represents the total number of DigiCoins a user currently holds. It's like a digital piggy bank keeping track of your DigiCoin wealth.
- Public Key: This publicly shared key acts as the receiving address for your DigiCoins. Think of it like a publicly known bank account number for receiving DigiCoin transfers from others.

Code Example (Illustrative Structure):

Elixir

```
defmodule Wallet do
  defstruct [:balance, :public_key]
end
```

This simplified code snippet showcases the structure of a Wallet module in Elixir. It defines two fields: balance to represent the user's DigiCoin holdings and public_key for receiving transactions and verification purposes.

Beyond the Basics

The concept of wallets extends beyond this foundational structure in real-world cryptocurrency systems:

- Implementation: Security is paramount. Real-world cryptocurrency wallets employ various techniques for secure storage of private keys. Hardware wallets that resemble physical USB devices and software wallets with robust encryption are common solutions to safeguard these critical keys.
- Advanced Features: Modern cryptocurrency wallets offer a range of functionalities beyond basic storage. Users can send and receive transactions, monitor their transaction history for better record-keeping, and even interact with decentralized applications (dApps) built on the cryptocurrency platform, opening doors to a wider ecosystem of possibilities.

Transaction Validation

Before a transaction involving DigiCoins is finalized and recorded, it must undergo a crucial process – validation. This acts as a security checkpoint, ensuring the integrity and fairness of the entire DigiCoin system.

Verifying Transaction Validity:

Imagine a meticulous accountant double-checking the books. Transaction validation performs a similar function. Here's what's typically involved:

- Balance Check: This ensures the sender has sufficient DigiCoins in their wallet to complete the transaction. You can't spend what you don't have! The system verifies if the transaction amount is less than or equal to the sender's current balance.
- Digital Signatures (Advanced Systems): In more sophisticated cryptocurrency systems, digital signatures add an extra layer of security. The sender signs the transaction with their private key, creating a unique digital fingerprint. The receiver can then use the sender's public key to verify the signature. This cryptographic verification ensures the transaction originated from the legitimate owner of the DigiCoins being sent.

Code Example (Simplified Validation):

Elixir
```
def validate_transaction(transaction, sender_wallet) do
  transaction.amount <= sender_wallet.balance
end
```

This simplified example demonstrates a basic validation check. It compares the transaction amount with the sender's wallet balance to ensure they have enough DigiCoins.

Transaction validation in real-world cryptocurrencies often involves a more complex process. Consensus mechanisms come into play, where participants in the network collaborate to reach an agreement on the validity of transactions. These mechanisms vary depending on the specific cryptocurrency but share the common goal of preventing unauthorized modifications and ensuring a secure and reliable network.

Remember: Secure storage of private keys and robust validation processes are fundamental for building trust and maintaining the integrity of your cryptocurrency system. By implementing these measures, you can create a secure environment for users to manage their DigiCoins with confidence.

9.3 Ensuring Network Security

The world of cryptocurrencies thrives on trust and security. In this section, we'll explore the critical security considerations specific to cryptocurrencies, ensuring your DigiCoin network operates like a digital Fort Knox.

The Double-Spend Dilemma: Preventing Coin Duplication

Imagine trying to spend the same dollar bill twice! This is a fundamental challenge in cryptocurrencies called "double-spending." Here's how we prevent it:

- Transaction Recording: Transactions involving DigiCoins need to be recorded securely and immutably (unchangeable). This typically involves a distributed ledger technology like a blockchain.
- Consensus Mechanisms: These mechanisms ensure all participants in the network agree on the validity of transactions and the current state of the ledger. Popular mechanisms include Proof of Work (PoW) and Proof of Stake (PoS).

Understanding Consensus Mechanisms (Simplified):

- Proof of Work (PoW): Imagine miners solving complex puzzles to validate transactions. The first miner to solve the puzzle gets to add the block of transactions to the blockchain. This system incentivizes miners to be honest, as adding invalid transactions wouldn't yield rewards.
- Proof of Stake (PoS): Think of it like a democratic voting system. Users who hold a stake (ownership) in the cryptocurrency can participate in the validation process. The more DigiCoins a user holds, the greater their influence in validating transactions. This approach aims to be more energy-efficient than PoW.

Sybil Attacks: Battling Fake Identities

Imagine a malicious actor creating a large number of fake accounts to gain control of the network. This is called a Sybil attack. Here's how to mitigate it:
- Reputation Systems: These systems assign a reputation score to each participant based on their

history of behavior. Users with a good reputation have more influence in the network, making it harder for fake identities to disrupt the system.

- Registration Requirements: Implementing registration processes with minimal barriers to entry while deterring fake accounts can be a balancing act. Techniques like requiring a small deposit of DigiCoins for registration can discourage Sybil attacks.

3. 51% Attack: Preventing Network Takeover

Imagine a single entity gaining control of more than half of the computing power in the network. This is a 51% attack, and it could allow the attacker to manipulate transactions or even reverse them. Here's how to make it harder:

- Cryptographic Hashing: Complex mathematical functions are used to create unique identifiers for transactions. Altering even a single bit in a transaction would drastically change its hash, making it easy to detect any tampering.
- Decentralization: The more geographically distributed a cryptocurrency network is, the harder it becomes for a single entity to gain control of 51% of the computing power. Spreading the network across various nodes across the globe enhances its security.

Code Example (Illustrative – Security Mechanisms are Complex):

While specific code for security mechanisms is beyond the scope of this chapter, imagine a module for validating transactions:

Elixir

```
defmodule DigiCoin.Security do
  def validate_transaction(transaction) do
    # ... (check transaction integrity using cryptographic
hashing)
    # ... (use consensus mechanism to verify transaction
validity)
  end
end
```

Staying updated on emerging threats and continuously evaluating the security posture of your cryptocurrency is essential. By implementing robust security measures and leveraging the power of Elixir's concurrency features, you can build a strong foundation for your DigiCoin network.

Chapter 10: Case study: Building Decentralized Applications with Elixir

This chapter dives into the heart of what makes blockchain technology so revolutionary. We'll explore how Elixir can empower you to build DApps that leverage the power of decentralization.

10.1 Developing DApps with Elixir

The world of Decentralized Applications (DApps) is booming, and Elixir is a powerful tool for bringing your DApp ideas to life. This section dives into the core aspects of DApp development with Elixir, equipping you to build applications that leverage the transformative power of blockchain technology.

Imagine applications that operate on a distributed network, free from central control. That's the fundamental concept behind DApps. Unlike traditional applications hosted on a single server, DApps run on a peer-to-peer network, like a blockchain. This distribution of data and logic across multiple devices fosters several advantages:

- Enhanced Security: Data stored on a blockchain is tamper-proof and transparent. This immutability strengthens security compared to centralized systems.

- Censorship Resistance: DApps are not under the control of any single entity. This resistance to censorship empowers users and fosters a more open and transparent application environment.
- Increased Trust: By eliminating the need for a central authority, DApps can promote trust and transparency between users interacting on the network.

Elixir's Role in DApp Development

Elixir's strengths make it an excellent choice for building robust and scalable DApps:

- Concurrency for Efficiency: Elixir's concurrency features are perfectly suited for handling the asynchronous nature of blockchain interactions. DApps often involve waiting for transactions to be confirmed on the network, and Elixir excels at managing these processes efficiently.
- Functional Programming for Clarity: Elixir's functional programming paradigm promotes code that is easier to reason about and maintain, crucial for complex DApp development.
- Rich Ecosystem of Libraries: The Elixir ecosystem offers a wealth of libraries specifically designed for blockchain interaction. Libraries like web3 or Ecto streamline communication with smart contracts and data retrieval from the blockchain.

The DApp Development Process

Building a DApp with Elixir typically involves these key phases:

- Conceptualizing the DApp: Define the purpose and functionality of your DApp. What problem are you trying to solve, and how will it leverage blockchain technology?
- Smart Contract Development (Optional): If your DApp requires specific functionalities on the blockchain, you'll need to develop smart contracts using a language like Solidity (for Ethereum) or RIDE (for Waves).
- Back-End Development with Elixir: This is where Elixir shines! Build the server-side logic of your DApp. This might involve handling user interactions, interacting with smart contracts, and managing data flow.
- Front-End Integration: Develop a user-friendly interface for your DApp. Popular frameworks like React or Phoenix.Live integrate seamlessly with Elixir to create a cohesive user experience.

Code Example (Illustrative - Data Fetching from Blockchain):

```Elixir
defmodule MyDapp.GetItems do
 use HTTPoison.Base
 def fetch_items do
  # ... (interact with blockchain node using HTTPoison library)
  # ... (retrieve data about available items)
  # ... (return the fetched data)
```

```
end
end
```

This simplified example showcases fetching data about available items from the blockchain. In a real-world scenario, you might use a library like web3 to interact with a specific blockchain network and smart contract.

10.2 Integrating Frontend Interfaces

The world of Decentralized Applications (DApps) is flourishing, and Elixir is a powerful tool for bringing your DApp ideas to life. This section dives into the core aspects of DApp development with Elixir, equipping you to build applications that leverage the transformative power of blockchain technology.

Imagine applications that operate on a distributed network, free from central control. That's the fundamental concept behind DApps. Unlike traditional applications hosted on a single server, DApps run on a peer-to-peer network, like a blockchain. This distribution of data and logic across multiple devices fosters several advantages:

- Enhanced Security: Data stored on a blockchain is tamper-proof and transparent. This immutability strengthens security compared to centralized systems.
- Censorship Resistance: DApps are not under the control of any single entity. This resistance to

censorship empowers users and fosters a more open and transparent application environment.

- Increased Trust: By eliminating the need for a central authority, DApps can promote trust and transparency between users interacting on the network.

Elixir's Role in DApp Development

Elixir's strengths make it an excellent choice for building robust and scalable DApps:

- Concurrency for Efficiency: Elixir's concurrency features are perfectly suited for handling the asynchronous nature of blockchain interactions. DApps often involve waiting for transactions to be confirmed on the network, and Elixir excels at managing these processes efficiently.
- Functional Programming for Clarity: Elixir's functional programming paradigm promotes code that is easier to reason about and maintain, crucial for complex DApp development.
- Rich Ecosystem of Libraries: The Elixir ecosystem offers a wealth of libraries specifically designed for blockchain interaction. Libraries like web3 or Ecto streamline communication with smart contracts and data retrieval from the blockchain.

3. The DApp Development Process: Breaking it Down

Building a DApp with Elixir typically involves these key phases:

- Conceptualizing the DApp: Define the purpose and functionality of your DApp. What problem are you trying to solve, and how will it leverage blockchain technology?

- Smart Contract Development (Optional): If your DApp requires specific functionalities on the blockchain, you'll need to develop smart contracts using a language like Solidity (for Ethereum) or RIDE (for Waves).
- Back-End Development with Elixir: This is where Elixir shines! Build the server-side logic of your DApp. This might involve handling user interactions, interacting with smart contracts, and managing data flow.
- Front-End Integration: Develop a user-friendly interface for your DApp. Popular frameworks like React or Phoenix.Live integrate seamlessly with Elixir to create a cohesive user experience.

Code Examples:

A. Data Fetching from Blockchain (Illustrative):

Elixir
```elixir
defmodule MyDapp.GetItems do
  use HTTPoison.Base
  def fetch_items do
    # Interact with a blockchain node using HTTPoison
    response =
HTTPoison.get("https://<blockchain_node_url>/items")
    case response do
      {:ok, %HTTPoison.Response{status_code: 200, body:
body}} ->
        # Parse the JSON response and extract item data
        items = Poison.decode!(body)
        {:ok, items}
```

```
    {:error, reason} ->
      {:error, reason}
  end
 end
end
```

This example showcases fetching data about available items from a blockchain node using the HTTPoison library. In a real-world scenario, you might use a library like web3 to interact with a specific blockchain network and smart contract.

B. Smart Contract Interaction (Simplified):

Imagine a DApp for a simple voting system on the blockchain. This example (focusing on concepts) demonstrates interacting with a smart contract function to cast a vote.

```
Elixir
defmodule MyDapp.Voting do
  # Assuming interaction with a deployed smart contract
  def cast_vote(voter_address, candidate_id) do
    # Interact with the smart contract's "castVote" function
{:ok, tx_hash} =
MySmartContract.castVote(voter_address, candidate_id)
    {:ok, tx_hash}
  end
end
```

This simplified example showcases calling a smart contract function named castVote using the voter's address and candidate ID. In a real-world scenario, you would likely use a library like web3 to interact with the smart contract and handle the transaction process.

By leveraging the power of Elixir and staying at the forefront of blockchain innovation, you can create DApps that revolutionize the way we interact with the digital world.

10.3 Showcasing Practical Use Cases of DApps

Decentralized Applications (DApps) are poised to disrupt numerous industries by enabling secure, transparent, and trustless interactions. Here's a glimpse into some captivating use cases that showcase the power of DApps in action, along with examples and illustrative code snippets:

1. Decentralized Finance (DeFi):

Imagine a financial system without centralized institutions like banks. DeFi DApps are making this a reality. Here's how:

- Peer-to-Peer Lending and Borrowing: DApps can facilitate borrowing and lending directly between users, eliminating the need for intermediaries and potentially offering more competitive rates.
- Decentralized Exchanges (DEXs): These DApps allow users to trade cryptocurrencies in a secure and

trustless manner, without relying on traditional exchanges. Here's a simplified code example (focusing on concepts) demonstrating a hypothetical DEX order placement:

```elixir
Elixir
defmodule MyDefiApp.Exchange do
  def place_order(user_address, token_to_sell, token_to_buy, amount) do
    # Interact with the DEX smart contract
    {:ok, tx_hash} = DexContract.place_order(user_address, token_to_sell, token_to_buy, amount)
    {:ok, tx_hash}
  end
end
```

- Yield Farming (Advanced): DApps can be used to participate in yield farming, a process of earning rewards on cryptocurrency holdings through DeFi protocols. However, it's important to remember that yield farming can involve complex financial instruments and carries inherent risks.

Example DApp: Uniswap is a popular DEX built on the Ethereum blockchain, enabling users to swap various cryptocurrencies directly with each other.

2. Supply Chain Management:

Imagine tracking the movement of goods throughout a supply chain with complete transparency. DApps can revolutionize this process:

- Immutable Tracking: Data about a product's origin, processing, and transportation can be stored on a blockchain, ensuring tamper-proof traceability. Here's an illustrative code snippet (focusing on concepts) demonstrating data storage on a blockchain:

Elixir
```
defmodule MySupplyChain.TrackItem do
  def update_location(item_id, new_location) do
    # Interact with the blockchain to store the updated location for the item
    # ... (using a library like Ecto to interact with the blockchain)
  end
end
```

- Enhanced Efficiency: DApps can automate tasks within the supply chain, streamlining processes and reducing errors.
- Consumer Trust: Consumers can gain greater confidence in the authenticity and ethical sourcing of products by tracking their journey on the blockchain.

Example DApp: VeChain is a blockchain platform specifically designed for supply chain management applications.

3. Decentralized Marketplaces: Empowering Peer-to-Peer Exchange

Imagine secure and trustless marketplaces where users can buy and sell goods directly with each other. DApps are making this possible:

- Escrow Services: Smart contracts can act as secure escrow agents, holding funds until certain conditions are met (e.g., successful delivery of goods). Here's a simplified code example (focusing on concepts) demonstrating initiating an escrow with a smart contract:

Elixir
```
defmodule MyMarketplace.Escrow do
  def create_escrow(buyer_address, seller_address, item_price) do
    # Interact with the smart contract to initiate an escrow for the purchase
    {:ok, escrow_address} = EscrowContract.create(buyer_address, seller_address, item_price)
    {:ok, escrow_address}
  end
end
```

- Eliminating Middlemen: DApps can facilitate peer-to-peer transactions, reducing transaction fees and empowering users.
- Wider Range of Applications: Decentralized marketplaces extend beyond physical goods. Imagine buying and selling digital assets like artwork or music directly from creators using DApps.

Example DApp: OpenSea is a leading marketplace for buying and selling non-fungible tokens (NFTs) representing digital ownership of unique items.

4. Social Media on the Blockchain

Imagine social media platforms where users control their data and can monetize their content creation. DApps are fostering this vision:

- Content Ownership: DApps can leverage blockchain technology to give users ownership of their data and content.
- Direct Monetization: Creators can potentially earn rewards directly from their audience without relying on advertising revenue models.
- Focus on Community: DApps can foster a more community-driven social media experience, empowering users and content creators.

Example DApp: Steemit is a social media platform built on a blockchain, where users can earn rewards for creating and curating content. However, it's important to note that Steemit has faced challenges in recent years, highlighting the evolving nature of the DApp landscape.

The potential applications of DApps are vast and constantly evolving. As blockchain technology matures and DApp development flourishes, we can expect to see even more innovative use cases emerge across various industries. Some exciting possibilities include:

- Decentralized Governance: DApps can be used to create more democratic and transparent governance models in organizations and communities.

- Identity Management: DApps can empower users to control their digital identities and securely share personal information with different applications.
- The Internet of Things (IoT): DApps can connect and manage a growing network of interconnected devices in a secure and decentralized way.

The DApp development landscape is rapidly changing. Stay curious, explore the latest advancements, and actively participate in the DApp development community. By leveraging the power of Elixir and embracing innovation, you can be part of shaping the future of decentralized applications.

Conclusion

As we reach the end of "Blockchain with Elixir: A Developer's Guide for Building High-Performance Blockchain Networks," it's essential to reflect on the journey we've undertaken and the knowledge we've accumulated. This book has aimed to provide a robust foundation in both blockchain technology and the Elixir programming language, equipping you with the skills needed to build scalable, secure, and efficient blockchain networks.

Throughout this book, we've explored the fundamental principles of blockchain technology, understanding how decentralized networks operate and the critical role of consensus mechanisms in maintaining trust and integrity. We've delved into the core components of blockchain systems, including nodes, ledgers, and smart contracts, and examined how these elements interact to create a cohesive and functional network.

We've also highlighted the unique advantages of using Elixir for blockchain development. Elixir's concurrency model, fault tolerance, and scalability make it an ideal choice for building robust blockchain applications. By leveraging the power of the BEAM virtual machine, Elixir allows developers to handle numerous simultaneous operations, ensuring that blockchain networks remain responsive and resilient under heavy loads.

The practical chapters of this book have guided you through the process of creating your own blockchain projects. From setting up a basic Elixir project to implementing complex features like smart contracts and consensus algorithms, you've learned how to translate theoretical concepts into working code. The case studies on building a cryptocurrency and developing decentralized applications (DApps) have provided concrete examples of how these technologies can be applied in real-world scenarios.

As we look to the future, it's clear that both blockchain technology and the Elixir language will continue to evolve. Emerging trends such as decentralized finance (DeFi), non-fungible tokens (NFTs), and advancements in scalability solutions like sharding and state channels will shape the landscape of blockchain development. Elixir, with its growing community and expanding ecosystem, will remain a valuable tool for developers seeking to innovate in this space.

The field of blockchain is dynamic and ever-changing. To stay ahead, it's crucial to engage with the broader community, participate in forums and conferences, and continuously experiment with new ideas and technologies. This book is just the beginning of your journey. The knowledge and skills you've gained here are foundational, but true mastery comes from ongoing practice and exploration.

In conclusion, building high-performance blockchain networks with Elixir offers a unique and rewarding challenge. The synergy between blockchain's transformative potential and Elixir's powerful features creates opportunities for groundbreaking applications and solutions. As you continue to develop your expertise, remember to approach each project with curiosity, creativity, and a commitment to excellence.

Thank you for embarking on this journey with us. We hope this book has been a valuable resource and that it inspires you to create innovative and impactful blockchain applications. Happy coding!

www.ingramcontent.com/pod-product-compliance
Lightning Source LLC
Chambersburg PA
CBHW082108220526
45472CB00009B/2098